OPTING IN

MOLLY FIORE

PEAKS OF EXCELLENCE

For Todd

You are my greatest teacher.
Thank you for the connection—for listening to me and
for getting me.

Acknowledgments

First and foremost I would like to thank the one person who has been with me through it all. During the ups and downs, the breakdowns and break-throughs, he has stood by me. Without him I would not be here. Thank you to my husband, TJ.

I would also like to acknowledge and thank my family. I love you all, more than you know. An added and special note to my nephew: he is my inspira-tion and will always hold a sacred place in my heart.

I could not complete this section without mentioning my girls. Thank you to my two best friends in the world. Torey and Amanda, I love you both. Thank you for being you, for your love, and your continued support.

Last, but not least, thank you to everyone who helped me in this journey, especially in producing the book. Mom, thank you for believing in me. Todd, thank you for the conversations and the unwavering stand. My Eagle County family, thanks to you all for listening, supporting, and encouraging. Sara Fabian and Landmark Education; Steve Chandler and the Coaching Prosperity School. Thank you to all my early readers. And a very special thanks to my editor, who pulled it all together and made it all possible, Charol Messenger.

Contents

Foreword

Have you ever thought about ending your life? You're not the only one. I have found myself feeling alone in the darkness, with no answers, no hope, and no light at the end of the tunnel, many times. In these times of complete despair, death seemed the only answer, the only escape. In fact, a year ago I came desperately close to ending my life. For so long, I had been unhappy, utterly lost, utterly alone. No one seemed to understand my struggle, nor the depth of my pain. No one got it. No one got me.

I obviously didn't end it that night. Instead, I made a choice in that dark hour to get busy living. This is my story of emerging from the darkness. This is my brutally honest and raw look at the darkest secrets that were keeping me a victim of my own life. This is the story of my year-long journey through the darkness into the light, my journey within.

Who is this book for? Anyone who feels "not gotten." Anyone who has ever felt alone, lost, hurt, confused, desperate. Anyone who is unhappy in his or her life. Anyone who feels lost in the darkness.

CHAPTER 1
Rock Bottom

"He who has a why to live can bear almost any how."
- Friedrich Nietzsche

I was staring at the blank Google page and, for the life of me, I could not figure out what to write in the search box. *I have hit rock bottom, please help me* was not bringing the results I was searching for. I felt so far down the rabbit hole that I knew I needed to check myself in somewhere: a mental hospital, rehab, or some other 24-hour living facility.

Option two: Give up. Opt out. Kill myself.

Even to me, that sounded desperate. But I *was* desperate.

How did I get here? I wondered vaguely. *How did I become so unhappy?*

I had a husband who loved me and a job I was proud to be part of. I had what is called a good life—yet it did not resonate with me at all.

I couldn't say this was *not* the life I wanted. That would require knowing what I did want. But I didn't know. I couldn't even articulate it. I knew only that I needed something else—to *feel* something else.

This was so impossible! How could I get myself out of this?

First, I was not sure I was in love with my husband, or if I even *wanted* to stay in the marriage. All the passion was gone. He was my best friend, but was that enough? Could I stay with him without passion and romance? I missed it! Was I settling? Would I regret staying? Would I regret leaving?

I didn't know. I felt an ache, a sickness, through my whole being. I wanted someone to take over my life, tell me what to do. I couldn't see a way out.

Second, I was in love with someone else. Third, that someone was my boss. This was a very big problem. I saw him every day. I felt things for him that I shouldn't— but I could not walk away from him.

I didn't want these feelings. I didn't ask for them. They haunted me. They would not let me go.

For months, I lay awake every night, next to my husband, obsessing about my boss Colin. What my life with him would be like. How it would feel to be with him. How it would feel to kiss him. I thought about making love to Colin, having kids with him. I could see having breakfast on a Saturday before one of our kids' soccer games.

Night after night, I lay awake with this dream.

Is this what I've been wanting? I asked myself, not knowing the answer. *If I leave my husband and marry Colin, will I be happy?*

If I could get a solid yes, I would do it! I would risk everything for the chance to be happy!

I hoped with the greatest desperation.

Why is this so difficult? I anguished. *Why don't I know what I want?*

As I lay in the darkness, I planned out my dream, the dream that would make me feel better.

How would I tell Colin how I felt? Did he feel the same? Could I leave my marriage? If I did, could I live with myself? I had given my word to my husband, TJ. I had committed. How could I go against that?

What would happen at work? I fretted. Would I have to quit, either way? Could Colin and I work together as husband and wife?

I obsessed, playing out as many different scenarios as I could imagine.

I am so disgusted with myself!

While eating dinner with TJ, I was thinking about Colin. TJ was talking, and I didn't hear a word. I was thinking, *What is Colin doing right now? Is he thinking about me?*

I'm losing my mind! This isn't real! I'm not being fair and true to my husband! There must be a way out!

TJ and I started going on dates. It didn't help that we lived two hours apart. Five months ago, I had moved two hours away to work for Colin.

The five previous years, as his office manager, had gone well, so it had seemed a good idea at the time. I would quit school, move back, and pick up where I'd left off ... settle back into my old job. I had no idea what I wanted to do with my life, anyway. In an attempt to find myself, I had enrolled back into college and was going for a degree in athletic training. After one month, I'd bailed out ... and that's when I got the call from Colin.

"Things are falling apart at the office," he said. "I'm not sure what I'm going to do."

I answered *yes* before I even realized what I was saying.

I then rationalized, to myself and to TJ: I could continue floundering in school, paying out money, or I could bring money in. I was doing this for Colin, I told myself and TJ. I'd known Colin a long time. He was a friend, like a brother. I couldn't say no.

So, four and a half days a week, I managed Colin's cardiology office and rented a small apartment nearby. On weekends, I went home to my husband and our black lab Lucy in our Rockwood trailer, parked in the back of the RV Ranch outside of Grand Junction, Colorado. I'd had this wonderful idea last year that TJ and I should sell our house and live in a travel trailer to save money. We'd tried to make our 31-foot travel trailer home in the trailer park. Our lot was just behind the office and next to the outdoor pool. On Sundays in the summer, they would have a pancake breakfast outside next to the office. It was our own little trailer-park community.

TJ and I had done this commuting thing several times throughout our marriage. It had always worked before, so why not now? At the time, it made sense.

Fast-forward five months. My feelings for Colin somehow changed from friend/brother to "in love."

TJ and I were on separate roller coasters. During the week, I was in work mode, doing my own thing. I worked out, watched TV (shows I wanted to watch), went out with friends—whenever I liked. I was on my own.

On Fridays, I went home to TJ—but I held back emotionally. I had been in my own space for five days. I couldn't just flip a switch and be all lovey-dovey. I couldn't go from nothing to hugging and kissing right away.

It took me to Sundays to transition to being close again to TJ. Just one problem. For him, it was the exact opposite. By Sunday, he was thinking of the week ahead and he was pushing me away.

It got so that I dreaded Fridays. TJ would want to hold my hand and constantly hug me. The more he did, the more I withdrew. I even cringed.

Irritated, I would tell him, "I need some space."

That only made him more clingy. Every time he reached for my hand, I pulled it away ... and felt guilty. I didn't want to hurt him. I felt like shit.

Our solution was a date night.

We went to a local Japanese restaurant. It was new. We could start fresh.

I did my best to be attentive and passionate. Tonight would be different. It had to be.

We walked in, holding hands. I was feeling closer. I had missed TJ this week. We shared a Japanese beer, Sapporo, and appetizers, pot stickers. I love the dipping sauce!

I started to relax. TJ talked about his week. Then my mind began to wander—back to Colin. He would be working late at the office.

Shit! Why am I thinking about Colin?

This had to stop. I had no idea what TJ was saying, because I was too busy obsessing about Colin.

My stomach hurt. I just wanted to leave. I pushed my food away and started crying.

TJ immediately stopped recounting his week. "What did I do?" he asked.

I started to answer. The tears really came then. I cried so hard that I could barely breathe. I put my face in my hands and just let it come. My entire body heaved.

Finally, I looked up, drained, and blew my nose. The concern on TJ's face just made me feel more terrible. "I'm in trouble," I squeaked out.

"What did you do?"

"I'm so unhappy."

"With what? Do you want to eat somewhere else?"

Oh, my god. He thought I didn't like the food. "I'm just so unhappy."

"What do we need to do to get you happy? Do you want to quit your job?"

Why was he so damn nice?

I shrugged. "I don't know. I just don't know anything."

"What's going on? Talk to me."

"I'm really confused about my feelings for Colin."

TJ frowned. His puzzled look embarrassed me.

"What do you mean?" he asked.

I couldn't look him in the eye. "I think I might be in love with Colin."

There it was. I'd said it. "I'm so confused about my feelings toward him."

TJ just looked at me. "When did this start?" he asked. "How long have you felt this way?"

Good question. *The truth?* I said to myself. *A long time.*

I realized I'd had feelings for Colin the moment I'd met him. He was so good-looking. On top of that, he was a surgeon, and he loved the outdoors. He was passionate about all the right things: hiking, skiing, the mountains.

I, on the other hand, was not such a package. I was in my twenties, trying to be somebody in the medical field. I had started five years earlier as a receptionist and was clawing my way up to manager. I was halfway through my MBA and desperately wanted to reach the top. I owned a condo and did a fair amount of skiing. Colin and I were both single and both looking for the right person in our lives. Or so I thought.

My manager had picked up on this immediately. She also happened to be my godmother and mentor in the business. She had taken a chance on me and had hired me straight out of college. I had worked in three other medical offices with her, and she had taught me everything she knew. I admired her and appreciated the confidence and respect she had from the community. I wanted to be a lot more like her. I wanted to go from where I was currently to management. I wanted to be on *her* level. I wanted the respect. I was willing to put my time in, and that's what I was doing. Putting in my time.

She immediately saw Colin as single and available. "He's perfect for you!" she declared.

I didn't want to let on that I agreed. "Oh, I don't know. I don't think so."

I absolutely wanted her to set me up with him. However, I was so scared. I didn't think he would like me, and being rejected would be devastating, so I played it cool.

"I talked with him," she confided, "and he wants help finding the right girl."

The smile on my face and the glow in my eyes were all she needed. She was on a mission.

Weeks went by and I got to know Colin. We talked often ... and I was definitely interested. Shy, yes. Terrified, absolutely.

There was no way I was going to make the first move. I couldn't. After each conversation, I had to report back to the matchmaker how things had gone.

I was starting to feel very uncomfortable and pressured to move faster and to be more aggressive than I ever had been. But she was my link in the business, and I didn't want to let her down.

However, I had no confidence in myself or faith that Colin would have any interest in me at all. He was so out of my league. So, I mustered up the courage one afternoon to ask him to go skiing with me. Easy. Common ground. Toward the end of the day, I asked what he was doing over the weekend.

"Oh, not much," he said. "What are you up to?"

"Want to take some runs together this weekend?" I asked, trying to play it cool, acting nonchalant.

"Oh, actually my friend from Denver is coming up to meet me," he said.

"Oh," I mustered. This was not going at all as I had hoped.

"We're going to hang out this weekend and ski in Vail," he said. "If you want to meet up with us and ski a run together, I would be okay with that."

Oh, my god! It would be okay if I tagged along? He saw me as his little sister. I was mortified. "Yeah, maybe," I muttered.

As we headed out for the day, I felt millimeters tall. I'd just made the biggest ass of myself. Seriously, my most humiliating moment. I was terrified to return to work.

Of course, my matchmaker was full of questions. "So, did you ask him out? What did he say? What are your plans? Tell me all about it."

My tears started to come. Rather than explain my pathetic response, I simply told her he'd said no.

She then started some serious backpedaling and she felt terrible. I said forget it ever happened, and she agreed. As far as I was concerned, it was over.

Then a year later, Colin hired me to run his practice.

I was hesitant, but figured I could put the past behind me. I put on my professional face, big time. I was seldom in a room alone with him, and I kept my distance. I didn't share my personal life. I was all business.

This worked -- at least, I thought it did. I worked for him for five years, without incident. We became good friends. The awkward start to our relationship was never mentioned.

I then began to wonder if he'd ever known I had feelings for him. Of course, at that point it really didn't matter. By then, I'd married TJ. Those old feelings for Colin were long buried.

I also decided that medical-office management was not for me, after all. I explained to Colin that I wanted to find something else. I needed a sense of purpose. I felt capable of more.

I stayed in touch with Colin, though. We talked now and then, and he kept me in the loop about the business. We had started his company together, and I had always treated it as if it were my own.

It was hard to let go. I even went to the office Christmas party after I quit. I was still close with a lot of the staff, and Colin still made me feel like a part of the team.

I started drinking along with everyone else, and got immersed in a drinking game of Jenga. When it's your turn, you have to take a drink and pull out one of the wooden blocks from the tower.

I successfully engineered a few turns and reached in to grab another block. Much to my relief, it easily slid out. However, the block's written message said, *Describe your most embarrassing moment.*

I instantly flashed back to asking Colin out. I hadn't thought about it in years. Now it was back—and crystal clear.

I looked up and Colin was looking right at me. "Well, what is it?" he asked.

I blanked. It was like he was seeing right through me. After a few moments, I made up something stupid.

It was then I started wondering about my old feelings. I decided to talk with Colin about it. Enough time had passed. I no longer worked for him, and I was married. Might as well clear the air. It was silly to have kept this bottled up for so long, I told myself. I could let it go. It was time.

Had he ever known how I felt? I wondered. Had that original conversation been the source of awkwardness between us? I hadn't ever really let him in.

Sitting in Colin's office, about to share with him how I'd felt all those years ago was terrifying. I chickened out.

I did tell him, though, about the office manager trying to set us up and how uncomfortable it had made me. Well, kind of true.

He smiled. "Yeah, I remember that. She was trying to set me up with you as well."

He went on to explain that he had just moved here and was terrified about starting a new business. He had felt the timing wasn't right to start a serious relationship, and he had left it at that.

But what Colin said next floored me. "You know," he said, "when we shook hands and agreed to work together, I thought we would end up married."

Are you kidding me? Suddenly, I was very confused. What did this mean? Had I missed the signals?

I'd thought the feelings were long gone. Plus, I was now married and he was in a relationship.

Okay, I could be grown up about this. I could let it go. It obviously wasn't meant to be.

Then Colin had called asking me to come back to work ... and it truly had felt okay, I thought. He was a friend, after all. It had been almost nine months since the big conversation, so things were different. The conversation had cleared the air. Now I could be more open with him.

I had been back to work for about three months and things were going well, or so I thought. It was late October and Colin almost took his own life. I almost lost him.

In that very small community, the incident was kept very quiet; only a few people knew. For a week, I showed up at work as if it were business as usual. I kept the practice running. I stayed strong.

But I was dying on the inside. I had almost lost Colin.

One day after work, I had to tell him. I called him and told him I needed to talk.

"Sure," he said, "let's talk tomorrow during lunch."

"This is going to be very difficult for me," I said. "I'm not sure I can do it at work."

"Okay, let's meet now."

He asked where we should meet. "How about my house?" I offered. However, I was renting a tiny little place and it was less than ideal. As I struggled to relay the directions, I changed my mind. "No, meet me at the office."

"Sure, I'll be right there."

My heart raced. What would I say to him? I felt so awkward. I had so many thoughts and feelings, a thousand things I wanted to say to Colin. What was okay? What wasn't? I didn't want to upset him.

Waiting for Colin to walk in the door was torturous. At the thought of possibly losing him, I didn't know if I was going to cry or throw up. I was shaken to the core. I had lost my older brother when I was in high school. I knew what true loss felt like. It was devastating. I had never gotten over my brother's death.

Colin walked in with his sister. She had flown in to support him through his crisis. It had never occurred to me that he wouldn't come alone.

My heart stopped. I had never met her. I was going to have a personal conversation with her here? I wanted to walk out.

Instead, I sat at the table in the break room. I had come here to tell Colin, and I was going to say it.

He sat next to me on the same side of the table. His sister took the chair across from us. She looked at me. They both waited.

I started to choke out the first few words, but started crying. I struggled to find my voice, embarrassed and vulnerable.

"I know this must be hard for you after what happened to your brother," Colin said.

Geez! Colin was thinking about *me*? He'd just tried to kill himself and he was concerned about *me*?

I took the Kleenex he handed me. "I can't believe I almost lost you," I mumbled. "You're ... you're like a brother to me. I already lost one brother without being able to say goodbye or tell him I loved him. I won't do it again. Colin, I love you. I can't imagine my life without you in it."

He pulled his chair closer to mine and took both of my hands in his. "I won't let that happen. I promise you. "

His sister stood. "You two have a lot to say to each other. I'll be in your office, Colin."

She left the room and I looked at Colin, into his eyes. I felt his love. I felt his love for me. I felt such a connection to him in that moment. In that moment, I was no longer alone.

For the first time, we shared our thoughts, our feelings, our fears. A weight lifted. I felt a peace within me. I could talk to Colin about anything!

His sister came back into the room and I got up to leave. As I walked past Colin, he hugged me. He held me. Tighter. He whispered into my ear, "I love you, too."

In this moment, my feelings for Colin became more, and an incredible love for him began to grow.

Over the next couple of months, Colin and I confided in each other, which brought us closer together than ever. I was confused. I tried to deny my feelings for him, but they became even more intense.

Soon, I couldn't stop thinking about him at all.

Now TJ knew. The whole story. What was I supposed to do now?

Sitting in the restaurant, I knew that my life would never be the same.

Back at home with TJ, I was a mess. I was between two worlds. I felt like a scab had been ripped off and I was bleeding. What now? What next?

TJ sat in the living room watching TV. His eyes were glazed over and I could tell he wasn't paying attention to the rerun of *Law and Order*. His face showed no emotion and he felt a million miles away.

In the bedroom, I called my other brother. Two years younger than me, Lee was the responsible one. It was late in the East where he lived, but this couldn't wait. I needed his advice.

As soon as I heard Lee's voice, I broke down. I could barely choke out the words.

"Molly, what's wrong?"

His voice was sluggish like he'd been sleeping.

"I'm in a really bad place."

"What's going on?"

Blubbering through my tears, I couldn't get out any coherent thoughts. "I don't know what I'm doing. TJ and I aren't doing well ... and my feelings for Colin ... I might be in love with him. Nothing in my life makes sense right now."

"Mol, just slow down. Slow down. I know that right in this moment everything seems dark and lonely. Trust me, it's not as bad as you may think. You are okay, and everything is going to be okay. All of this can be worked out."

That seemed to help. I started to see that maybe there was no need for panic. We hung up with an agreement to talk in the morning. My brother Lee would help me get through this.

I sat on the bed, and a deep fear started to spread through me. I was jeopardizing my marriage. TJ was my rock. Without his stability and support, I would have nothing.

What the fuck am I doing!

I needed another voice of reason, someone to help me through this night.

Sweet TJ drove me to Sophia's, one of my closest friends. TJ insisted. He knew that if I went alone, I might never return home. There was still no emotion on his face. He was stone cold, gripping the steering wheel so tightly that his knuckles turned white.

As he drove us across town, he reached for my hand. I looked at him. He was pale with worry. I didn't know if I could love him as he deserved.

I couldn't stay with TJ, and I couldn't leave him. I didn't know why.

I couldn't love Colin this way, either. What was the answer?

I thought about Colin's recent suicide attempt, and a calm came over me. Maybe that was my answer?

The thought of giving up on life gave me a surge of relief. I finally pulled in a breath of air.

As TJ drove, a silence weighed on us, a numbness. I became numb to my life.

I told Sophia about Colin and TJ. How I was so lost and so tired.

TJ sat in the background, taking it all in. I was lost in my own misery. It was all about me, as it had been for quite some time.

Suddenly, I was so tired. I just wanted to close my eyes and disappear.

Sophia asked if I wanted to go to the hospital. What a strange question.

I found myself answering "Yes." I needed someone to take over, to tell me what to do.

TJ and Sophia started a whirlwind of activity. They made calls, searched the internet, called my insurance. I guess finding a mental-health facility is harder than just deciding to check yourself in.

"You guys spend the night," Sophia offered. "I'll call Colin and tell him you need some time. We'll get through this."

"Okay."

What else could I do? I would make it through the night. I couldn't think of anything else to do. It was all I could do to take another breath.

.

CHAPTER 2
Disconnected

"Failure is not fatal. Only failure to get back up is."
- John C. Maxwell

I don't know if I slept or not. I passed the night in a numb haze. Disconnected. From myself. From the world.

I did feel better knowing that two people in the world had heard my darkest thoughts—and still loved me. That was a start.

The next morning, I felt relief. Also, total embarrassment. The way I had fallen apart. The way I had treated my husband. The words I had said.

I was better than this! This was not the person I knew myself to be. Something was very wrong. I knew I needed help, but could I feel better? Was it even possible?

I walked downstairs at Sophia's to find TJ cooking me breakfast. He must have slept on the couch. I had awakened in my clothes from the night before, on top of Sophia's guest bed.

"You need to eat," TJ instructed.

It broke my heart. I had told him less than twenty-four hours earlier that I loved another man. Yet TJ still loved me, and he was putting my needs before his. I wanted TJ to get mad, yell—*not* be nice. It made me feel even worse.

Sophia walked in, all business. "What's your plan for today?" she asked.

"Keep breathing," I answered, only half kidding.

I had no plan. So, I started with what I knew. I called my family doctor. I gave her a brief synopsis over the phone about what was going on and asked what I should do.

She told me to come in immediately, right after lunch. TJ and Sophia both agreed that I should go alone. He was such a mixed-up part of this equation.

After their reassuring and supportive hugs, I headed to my appointment early. I needed time to get my thoughts together.

While driving there, I weighed everything—and decided that I should leave TJ. If I really loved him, the way he deserved, the way a wife should, I would not be filled with such doubt. I must get a divorce.

Yet, at the thought of leaving TJ, no longer having him in my life, panic swept through me and I sobbed. I could barely catch my breath. As I continued to drive, I wiped the tears from my face.

"This is ridiculous!" I chastised myself.

I showed up at the doctor's two hours early, a wreck, my eyes red and puffy. I was still streaming tears, my nose so full of snot that I could barely breathe. I used the entire box of tissues in the waiting room as I cried and cried, bent over in anguish. I didn't care who saw me.

I consumed the doctor's entire lunch hour. Either it was pity or she couldn't tolerate a patient having a complete meltdown in her waiting room.

I sorted through my conflicted feelings, for Colin, for my husband, how lost I felt.

She heard me out. Then came her diagnosis: bipolar.

Oh?

I didn't hear anything she said after the word *bipolar.*

She explained the highs and lows and extreme behaviors. She mentioned compulsive behavior. She told me her thoughts and scheduled an appointment with a psychologist. She also mentioned that it would be helpful for me to go online and take a survey on bipolar behaviors.

I was relieved that there might be a reason for my strange behavior. Maybe my brain was flawed? So that's why I had sunk so low in my life? Maybe I wasn't a complete failure, after all? There was hope. I had hope!

I just needed counseling and medication. So, I decided to give my divorce decision more thought. Better to get mentally balanced before making such a major life change.

With my new perspective, seeing things more clearly, I decided I needed a break, some time to sort through this new concept—bipolar. I could go to my brother Lee's. Christmas was a week away. He would be off work. I could relax at his house. He was the one to help me through this.

My plan? Drive straight through across country. Get there just days before Christmas.

My spirits began to lift. The thought of a hug from my brother brought such relief! I felt so much lighter! Going to Lee's for Christmas was fun to think about. I clung to that plan like a sliver of light in a dark tunnel.

What about TJ? Should I go alone? I could use some time to figure out what I wanted. Would this be running away from the problem? I went back and forth. I could fly, but it might be hard to get a ticket at the last minute over the Christmas holiday. A road trip would be long but therapeutic.

As I thought of all the scenarios, all the options, and everyone involved, the decision came down to one thing. Regardless of everything else, what did I want? What would make me happy?

Easy. I wanted to drive to my brother's—with TJ and my black lab. The thought of us all together on a road trip made me smile.

While driving back to Sophia's, I called my brother Lee on my cell phone and he was as excited as I was.

"Mol, that would be awesome! It will be fun to have us all together. Yes, of course, come."

Beaming, I then called TJ at his job as an oil-and-gas engineer. I couldn't wait until tonight. I was exhilarated by my news from the doctor and my new plan.

"I want to go with you," TJ said enthusiastically before I even had the chance to ask him.

"Yeah, I want you to," I said.

I could feel TJ smiling through the phone. The light got a little brighter. I was ready to hit the road!

One more call to make. Colin. I needed to ask for the time off to be gone over Christmas. I was nervous to tell him. I took a deep breath and sucked in as much courage as I could muster.

"Hey, Mol. How are you feeling?" Colin asked, our first chat since my flake-out.

"Better," I replied.

"Sophia told me that you and TJ are having problems?"

"Yeah. It's complicated."

Bottom line, Colin encouraged me to take as much time as I needed to get healthy and find the answers I was looking for. I appreciated his support; however, it felt awkward not to mention that he had so much to do with all of this.

On the road, everything slowed down. TJ drove and I relaxed, as much as I could. The miles rolled by and by, and my mind began to wander. Lucy curled up in the back on her dog bed. She looked so at peace, so at ease, and I felt myself wishing for such contentment.

My dark secrets had not turned away those I loved. Maybe things weren't as bad as I thought? Maybe I wasn't such a terrible person after all?

I had prided myself on living by high standards and integrity. It tore at my core that I had feelings for a man who was not my husband.

TJ and I drove long stretches without much conversation. He would drive four or five hours, then we would switch.

I found the road healing. With each mile, I felt more at ease. I didn't have answers, but that now felt more acceptable. It felt okay not knowing, at least for now.

We decided to drive straight through and not stop. We were both really enjoying the time behind the wheel and we wanted to keep going.

Since we hadn't planned on being with my brother and his family for Christmas, we didn't have any presents. So, we bought one gift at each gas station along the way. It was a fun game that had both of us laughing—a very good thing.

With our treasures, ranging from MoonPies to cigarette lighters, we rolled into New Hampshire. It was like coming home from college. The house was decorated, and my brother, sister-in-law, and nine-year-old nephew welcomed me and TJ with open arms. Lucy immediately ran into the house and checked out their yellow lab's dog toys and food bowl. It felt good to be with family.

My nephew took a look at our numerous small packages and enthusiastically offered, "Do you guys need help carrying in the presents?"

TJ and I looked at each other and burst out laughing, full of joy.

TJ and I had talked about sleeping arrangements on the drive out. Our relationship had more questions than answers. Nevertheless, we agreed to share my brother's one spare bedroom, and share the bed, but leave it at that. Things were complicated enough without adding sex. Lucy would sleep on the floor beside us.

Over the next few days, I regained my energy and found my holiday spirit. TJ and I both spent time with my nephew, sledding, eating, watching movies, and of course shopping.

Christmas traditions and time with my family were a distraction, but Colin was still on my mind. I still struggled with what to do.

In time, I decided: Come clean with Colin. No more hiding. No more pretending. Let the cards fall where they may.

So, one night after dinner, I went up to the spare bedroom, sat on the edge of the bed, and called Colin. I stared out the window at the neighborhood streetlight, feeling cold as I listened to each ring, one after another. Colin didn't answer, and I was unable to leave a message. *A sign from Above*, I decided. *Or not.*

Actually, I felt relief that Colin didn't pick up. Well, initial relief. Then the worry was back. So, I e-mailed him.

> Colin, I've tried to call a few times. I need to talk to you. I want to tell you what's on my mind, and I can't wait. I need for you to know now.
>
> When we talked the other night, I didn't give you the whole story. I need to explain.
>
> The truth is my feelings for you have gotten very confused. When I first started working for you, I, too, thought (or hoped) that one day we would end up together. I just never got the impression that you felt that way, too. So, I buried my feelings. Now, to learn, so many years later, that you felt similar at one point seems so unfair.
>
> I haven't done the best job of processing my feelings. In fact, I've done a very poor job over these past few months, and my marriage has suffered. I've taken a step back, and I now see that I need to act with loyalty and to honor my marriage. I also need to respect the relationship you are in. So, I need to walk away from the business. I know I made a commitment to you for the business. I will do my best to honor that.

I was hoping to talk with you about a plan to leave the practice the right way. I absolutely want to do the right thing.

Sorry you are reading this, rather than hearing it from me. I needed for you to know the truth. I don't want to hurt anyone, especially not you. I hope you understand. I'll wait to hear from you.

Molly

Well, it was out. No way to reel it back in.

I was actually relieved, free from shame and the feeling that I hadn't been honest. Concealing my feelings had felt like lying.

However, I did worry about Colin's reaction. I didn't want him completely out of my life. A part of me would always love him, but now I realized I didn't want to spend my life with him. Something was missing with him. Something was off. I couldn't put my finger on it exactly. It just didn't feel right. So I accepted my fate that the opportunity to be with Colin had passed and we wouldn't be together. He wasn't meant to be in my life, not in that way. Deep down, I also knew I didn't love Colin in that way. If I was honest with myself, the only man I truly loved was TJ.

So in this moment, I chose TJ. I *wanted* to be in the marriage -- not by default, but because of a deep genuine love.

I lay awake in my brother's spare bedroom, next to TJ, with Lucy snoring on the floor beside us. The streetlight was bright and shining into the room.

Many times, I looked over at my laptop, tempted to check my e-mail. *No. I must shed this obsessive behavior.*

I didn't sleep well. I tossed and turned, thoughts running through my mind. What would my life be like without the job? Would Colin remain in my life in any way? Could my marriage survive this? *Was* I bipolar? Would this madness subside? Was an imbalance in my brain causing this mania? Would medication ease it? So many questions. I drifted.

I woke up alone. TJ must have headed downstairs for coffee. As I opened my eyes, I gazed at the computer. It was reasonable to check my e-mail. That was normal, I told myself.

Anxiety spread through my body. Just then, the computer woke out of its own sleep and the light streamed into the room. So, I logged on.

Hi Mol, I'm sorry we couldn't connect today. My phone was the issue. From one until five I couldn't make or receive calls. Then I had to run to the hospital.

Anyway, thanks for being upfront and keeping me informed. I am certainly disappointed to hear you must leave. I guess I understand your reasons, but I have mixed feelings over all of this, as I am sure you do, too.

Molly, we need to talk about this. There is too much to say to put it in an e-mail, but I need to say a couple of things now. First, I respect your decision. I'm not happy about it, and I think TJ is being selfish keeping you away from your career and from me. But I respect your marriage and your commitment to him.

Second, the you and me thing. Yes, when you and I walked away from Starbucks that day, agreeing to put this business together, I thought you and I would get together. Yes, I kept those feelings from you and, yes, it never happened.

Then as we got the business going, it never seemed appropriate for me to date you. I tried to run the business with integrity, and I felt that meant no dating of my staff. What a slippery slope that would have been, I thought.

Looking back, I feel it was a catch-22. I could never know if it would work between us unless we tried, but we shouldn't try unless we really knew it would work.

As much as we ran the practice together, ultimately I was your boss. Could I call myself an honorable person if I dated someone whose paycheck I signed? As I struggled with this issue, it seemed like when you were single I was dating someone, and vice versa. When TJ came along for you, I felt the issue was decided for me. You were never single again.

I guess what I'm trying to say is, yes, you and I have always had these feelings for each other and, yes, we never had the opportunity to act upon them. Yes, that doesn't seem fair, and life often isn't fair.

You and I are of the same mold when it comes to fidelity and commitment. As close as I feel to you, I would never come between you and TJ. At this point in our lives, I am not allowed, by the rules of honor and integrity, to have any romantic feelings for you. I have accepted this. It sounds like you continue to struggle with it, however. If this is the case, then yes, you need to leave this job. It kills me to lose you a second time, but the truth is I lost you a long time ago.

Lastly, thank you, Molly. You have been a huge part of my life since I moved here. I doubt that I could have made it here without you. You put me solidly in my place here. You set me up to succeed here.

More recently, you literally saved my life. For all of this, I thank you. I can never fully repay you for all that you have done. As it did when you left before, it will hurt me again to see you leave but, once again, I will survive. I hope our friendship also will survive.

The practice can run without you, but I'm not sure I can. I hope and pray that you do not leave my life, and I hope that you, TJ, and I can continue our friendship together.

From my end, I will start looking into my options. From your end, please know that I need you for a little while longer. We will need to work together on this. I will do my best to expedite this transition, if you feel like this is necessary, but I do need you to stay on for now. Please do not leave me hanging, but let me know what you do need time wise.

Tomorrow, I am free all afternoon and, hopefully, my phone will work. If not, I'll e-mail you again.

I hope you are feeling better, Molly. I want you to be happy. You deserve it. You have my respect and you will always have my friendship. Let's talk soon

Colin

Colin didn't hate me! Also, my feelings weren't ridiculous, after all. Somehow, it made me feel better to know how he had felt, too. Maybe I wouldn't have to leave the job? I contemplated. Nothing had been done that couldn't be repaired. Maybe I could continue to work for Colin *and* dedicate myself to my marriage *and* be the person I wanted to be?

I called Colin that afternoon. Suddenly there was an awkward distance between us. After a few stumbles, we discussed the office logistics.

Again, he emphasized that he didn't want me to leave him without help. It stung that he thought I would. I had spent the last five years providing my loyalty. I wouldn't bail on him. I wouldn't do that to him or the staff.

We decided I would go back to work after Christmas and test the waters. We would both give our best effort to work together professionally. We would establish boundaries. We would not cross the line.

Christmas morning arrived and I gleamed as my nephew ripped open his presents.

It had been several days since I had spoken to Colin. I felt good about my decision to return to work, and I knew I wanted to spend my life with TJ.

I found myself engrossed in a game with my nephew. Hours passed without a thought of Colin. I was getting my life back, and myself back. The little voice in my mind had quieted, at last. At least for now.

CHAPTER 3
The One Thing

"A journey of a thousand miles must begin with a single step."
- Lao Tzu

My life felt full of possibilities. I had a clean slate.

The thoughts that had run my life for the last few months were gone. I showed up at work authentically as Colin's friend and employee. No more secrets.

I still thought about him. I wondered about his Christmas. However, the emotions were no longer intense. The thoughts came, but they no longer controlled me. It was the new year. I had a fresh start.

I needed a new strategy, a plan to propel myself out of my depression. Something that would help me get back to the basics of who I really was. I would reprioritize. I would get healthy.

One. Exercise. One gym workout per week. Five times weekly, thirty minutes of sit-ups, pushups, physical therapy for my chronic back pain, two outdoor activities per week.

Two. Eat healthy. Well-balanced meals. Buy groceries by the week. Make lunches to take to work.

Three. Read. Thirty minutes every day. Stick with one book. Fun reading, too.

Four. Keep a journal. Every day for forty days. I'd write in my journal ten to fifteen minutes every day. For Christmas, I'd received *40 Days and 40 Nights: Taking Time Out for Self-Discovery* by Ilene Sagalove. The back of the book promised, "A guided journal to support and inspire you as you take your own symbolic 40-day excursion into self-inquiry, personal discovery, and conscious growth."

Five. Get counseling. Commit.

Six. Heal my marriage. Work through the book *Love Dare*, fifteen minutes every day.

I was on a roll. I had a plan. It felt good to get up in the morning with a sense of purpose—and I was determined. I did my fitness routines. I checked off the days in my journal. I felt really good. Maybe this was what I'd needed all along? I'd just needed a plan.

Going back to work, I was very nervous walking in the door. The staff knew I was having problems. They thought it was only that I'd had too much on my plate. They didn't know the details. They didn't know how I'd felt about Colin.

I was also very nervous about still working with him. Could I do it? Would the feelings still be there? Would I honor my commitments to myself?

It wasn't nearly as bad as I expected. The staff were gracious and caring. Though things with Colin were certainly awkward, it felt good to get back to work and focus on something besides myself.

I was embarrassed about what he might be thinking of me, and wondered if he had lost confidence in me. However, these thoughts no longer consumed my days. Instead, I sought to find my stride with Colin and to develop a positive working relationship.

Once I realized there was no need for shame or embarrassment, I started thinking about other areas of my life. Telling the truth about my feelings for Colin had brought me peace. There was a freedom in being honest.

Where else in my life was I holding back? I wondered. Where else could the truth set me free? What were my darker secrets that I was keeping from myself, the ones lurking deep down that I didn't want to face?

Sitting at the tiny breakfast table in my personal apartment in Colorado, after work one night I looked into the dark corners of my mind. At first, I drew a blank and laughed at my self-consciousness.

It's safe, I whispered to myself.

So I admitted my ugly truth and poured it into my journal:

I feel ugly. I never thought anyone would want to marry me. I've always felt damaged, unwanted, unlovable.

I'm not smart. Since the second grade, I've been the dumb kid hiding out in a nerd suit. I work so hard to keep up the façade. My dad believes I'm smart, but it's a role I play. The truth, I'm not smart.

I don't have integrity. I'm a cheater. I cheated on every boyfriend I ever had. I think about other men, men who are not my husband. I don't want anyone to know how immoral I really am.

Amazing what comes out when you start writing. I'd had no idea I felt these things. How could I possibly find peace and freedom? This was the path to authenticity?

I thought more about it. *Why* did I think about other men? Why *wasn't* TJ's love enough? Why did I look for more? Why did I want Colin's attention? Why did I want him to love me? Why did I crave it? Why did I feel I must have it?

I wanted to feel special. I also realized, I liked the challenge. Men became less appealing once I had their attention. It seemed to be true of TJ. Maybe it would be true of Colin?

I needed to stop this. I needed to seek my own approval, not others'. How could I do that?

I thought about what had made me feel proud of myself. I had completed several triathlons and several college degrees, a BA in Biology and Environmental Studies as well as an MBA. I was proud of my family and friends ... and my honesty.

Then I realized that I needed to be proud of myself again. How could I find my way back? I needed help. Counseling. There *was* something wrong with me. Maybe I *was* bipolar?

I hoped that was the answer. *Please help me out of the rabbit hole!* I cried in desperation.

I looked around. Most people seemed okay, content with who they were. Why wasn't I? Why was it so hard for me to be happy?

I had promised TJ. I wanted to honor my word. I owed him this. I wanted to repair the damage.

I didn't go into counseling with an open mind. I had tried it three times in the past, and each time had left me feeling even more miserable.

The first time, I was a misfit in college, a nerd, and away from home. Then a friend died.

OPTING IN

A bunch of us were partying one night and couldn't find him. Then there he was, lying dead in a driveway. We couldn't feel a pulse. CPR did nothing. He was gone. His death leveled me. I had already lost my older brother.

I had terrible nightmares, which haunted me throughout that day. I'd thought I was tough. I tried to suck it up, but the fear wouldn't go away. Counseling was a sign of weakness. But I was barely holding on, so I stooped so low as to seek help.

It didn't go well. The session felt like a police interrogation. I went to the counseling service at the school, and it never occurred to me they would have a conflict of interest. As I explained about my friend's death, the counselor perked up. He wanted details. He kept asking about the specifics of the accident. He took notes and wrote down everything I said. In the pit of my stomach, I felt something wasn't right. I got up right then and never went back. *Fuck counseling!*

The second time I tried counseling, I had just dropped out of physician assistant school and realized I had no sense of personal identity. I had lived my entire life making other people happy. My physician had suggested I see someone, so, true to form, I did as I was told.

Again, it did not go well. I went one time. It started out with simple background information, and I explained my decision to quit school. He asked about my parents and siblings, if I was the oldest child.

I had always struggled with this question. The oldest? No. My big brother had that honor. I explained that he had died when I was in high school.

An uncomfortable silence followed. The therapist asked about the counseling I'd received after my brother's death. I hadn't had any counseling. His eyes lit up and he wrote down all kinds of stuff in his notebook. We never got past that. No, I had never talked to anyone professionally about my brother's death. "I thought you guys were supposed to be good

35

listeners," I pretty much said. "Shit, this is ridiculous." And I walked out.

My last and final shot was marriage counseling. This didn't go much better. TJ and I went a few times. It seemed to help our communication, so I changed my tune about counseling. Maybe I'd just had a few bad experiences, I figured.

My open mind didn't last long. By our third visit, I was concerned that our insurance hadn't paid any of our claims. I had previously asked the counselor to make sure she was contracted. She had assured us she was, but said we had to submit the claims.

This was what I did for a living, so no problem. However, the insurance wasn't paying. I then learned that the counselor recently had left the company we thought we were working with, and she was on her own; she wasn't contracted with any insurance companies. In addition, her name had not yet been removed from the company or insurance websites. She had lied. When I confronted her, she said I must have misunderstood. *Fuck counseling!*

Now here I was again. Smarter this time, I hoped. I confirmed the insurance and got a referral. I would not be suckered a *fourth* time.

I went in wanting to believe, but I decided something the moment I walked into the office. I would not talk about the death of my brother, period. I was sick of people assuming they had me figured out. Not this time.

That was my mistake. Withholding certain experiences did not make for an open and honest trust between us. Maybe I didn't want the counseling to work?

The first session was a disaster. I was a spaz. I merely condensed what had occurred over the past few months: my feelings for my boss, my husband, how I wanted to keep my job, and, oh, that I might be bipolar but I didn't think so. I tried to sound sane.

By the time I finished my story, our time was up. I felt like I'd just thrown up all over his office. Instead of feeling better, I felt crazier ... and that something most definitely was very wrong with me.

I was just about over the funk of this first appointment when a week had passed and it was time for the second. Maybe now that I had thrown all my cards on the table, so to speak, we would get somewhere, I figured.

We didn't. First, I was embarrassed. I felt very uncomfortable and very judged. I already felt low enough about myself. This just dragged me lower.

He kept questioning my feelings for Colin and alluding to how inappropriate that was, since I was married.

Well, no shit! Why do you think I'm here? I felt like saying.

We started this vicious cycle, him questioning my behavior, me justifying myself.

As much as I didn't want to quit on therapy, again, I couldn't stomach seeing this guy one more time. "I'm healed," I said. "You did such an amazing job that I don't feel bad anymore. I feel really good about my situation, and I don't really have anything else to talk about with you."

I wasn't that blatant, but that's the gist of it. He said that was fine, to call him if I needed him again.

Sure, buddy, sure thing.

Counseling crossed off the list! I would find another way to self-respect.

Some days I felt great, full of energy. Others, I couldn't pull myself out of bed. One thing kept me moving forward. Exercise. I just felt better when I exercised! It made me feel very motivated.

On days that it was a struggle, I pushed through, I made myself do it. The first few miles or minutes were quite painful. Then my mood changed—and I lit up. That's when I knew—this was the one thing.

This period in my life was all about taking note. I was on a quest to be happy, sick and tired of feeling sick and tired. Pain and suffering had been my norm. I didn't want that anymore. I wanted something else.

CHAPTER 4
The Big Dream

"Daring to dream means daring to live." - Robert H. Shuller,
Success Is Never Ending and Failure Is Never Final

I was already off track.

I promptly blew off my new plan to eat healthy, get good nutrition, work out (including stretches and exercise for my low-back pain), and write every day.

I watched three hours of *The Bachelor*, while consuming an entire bowl of popcorn, a bag of Skittles, a burrito, carrots, and celery. So much for my healthy diet. Did the carrots and celery count?

Why did I turn on the TV? I always felt bad after, like I was wasting my time.

No more TV this week! I vowed. *Not one more night!*

Then I sat through the entire *Wings of Love* saga.

Finally, I did get up and go to the gym, to work off the Skittles. I didn't feel like going. I forced myself, dragged my feet.

When I walked in, and saw the same people on the same machines, I almost walked back out. How did they do it every day, the same thing over and over?

Nevertheless, I tossed my jacket and sweat pants into a locker, then decided to weigh myself. *Uh-oh!*

I forced myself onto a treadmill. There was no ignoring that I really had to be here.

When I hit the 3.0 speed mark, I looked over at the super-skinny girl who was barely sweating at 7.5. *Shit!*

I walked for five minutes, then convinced myself I could run for twenty. I could do anything for twenty minutes, I told myself.

I had trouble getting to 6.0, but I did manage the twenty minutes! Plus, back and leg stretches. That should have melted away five or six Skittles, I figured. One more day at the gym—done!

The next day, I told myself that after work I would read, journal, and write. I did none of these. I had a wicked headache and I just wanted to close my eyes.

I left work early, rare for me. I started to watch some TV (I know) and decided to just go to bed. I immediately passed out and didn't stir until the phone rang at 5:30 a.m. TJ was spoiling me, with wake-up calls when I was away from home. I guess that was the point.

"Hi, love!" he said cheerfully.

"What time is it?"

"5:30 a.m."

"In the morning?"

After a few minutes to wake up, I felt refreshed and ready for a new start, and I re-dedicated myself to my plan.

Number one. Change my attitude.

I had always seen myself writing a book *in the future*. Time to change that. The time was *now*. If I wanted to achieve success, I needed to see the book as already finished and published.

I started writing.

Writing had been on my mind, on my bucket list, my to-do list, my wish list, my one-day list for as long as I could remember. Now it was time. 5:53 a.m., five months after I returned to work with Colin. I would start writing *now*.

Writing had come to me as an epiphany. I had seen myself traveling the country and giving motivational speeches.

Just one problem. I stared at a blank computer screen. Now what?

All I could think was, I am very average. I aim for great, but can an average person make it? Could I really succeed as a writer? Or was I reaching too far? Were *Oprah* and *Ellen DeGeneres* beyond my reach?

So as I stared at my computer screen, wondering what to do, I gave it some deep thought. Why did I want to write a book, anyway? Why did I feel I must? Answer: to make a difference, to be of value, to change lives.

I would travel the United States, with TJ, on a mission, teaching people how to be everything they wanted to be. I could do that. I was doing that.

Respect, to be sought after, for people to *want* to talk to *me*. There it was. I wanted to be important. I wanted to matter.

This book was my *Julie Julia*, my *Eat, Pray, Love*. I would give it a year. I could write a book in a year.

Watching TV had resulted in my feeling lazy. If I wanted a different out-come, I needed to make huge changes. I would write, read, research, join meetings, walk, meditate, go out to dinner, cook, clean, go to movies, just relax at home, and watch TV only one night a week. This was more in line with my new self!

I am in control, I affirmed.

However, underneath my bravado I honestly felt it was too late for me to dream. I didn't have a passion burning in me, like others I had watched succeed—doctors, singers, actors, athletes. Why didn't I? Johnny Cash, for example, knew he loved singing from the time he was born.

I had never had a burning desire for anything. Why not? Was there some-thing wrong with me? *Was* I born to do something special? If so, what was it?

Doubt plagued me. Always had. While others had gone on to their dream jobs, I had floundered. Now, I was thirty-four. Too late.

I had missed medical school, missed becoming a marine biologist (so no work at Sea World), didn't start training to be a ski racer at two years old. I had missed the boat.

There is a passion in me! I argued with myself. *I know there is, somewhere. I just need to find it. I must believe it's not too late.*

That's what my new plan was all about. I just had to change my response, and the change in outcome would follow.

The TV thing *was* a challenge. After work every day, when I walked in the door at six p.m., I was hungry and tired. I just wanted to plop on the couch, with something quick and easy to eat, and watch TV.

How about a compromise? I told myself. I clicked on the TV. I would watch *one* program while eating dinner, at the kitchen table.

I cycled through the channels and found a documentary on Bill Gates. Ah, something educational.

I watched a half hour, then I clicked it off. Success!

I told Sophia about my writing a book. Part of me wanted to keep it a secret, then surprise everyone with a finished copy. That sounded good, but I knew that if I didn't tell anyone it was because I wouldn't want them to see me fail.

Sophia was intrigued. She wanted details. How and why had I decided to do this?

We were on our way to a movie, so I gave her the Cliff Notes version. I explained my grandiose ideas. Then I laughed nervously. "Am I kidding myself?"

"Oh, girl, no."

"I convinced myself I could do this. But when I say it out loud, it just sounds like a pipe dream."

"Listen to me," she said seriously, "you are doing it already. You are writing a book. You get that? You are writing a book."

"I really am, aren't I?"

"You know you are."

"I really do want it," I confessed.

"How will you see it through?" she asked.

"What do you mean?"

"Well, there are many things I've wanted to do. I'd start out with all this energy, then it would just die out."

"I know what you mean."

"I really want to know how you stay dedicated. I want that secret!" She smiled.

"I think what drives me is I need to know why I am here, what I was put on this earth to do. That's what this book is about for me. Maybe by writing it, I'll find my purpose and that will make me happy?"

"Just remember, I'm always here for you, sister."

I smiled and gave Sophia a hug. She always said just the right thing.

Telling Sophia gave me accountability. Knowing she cared also made me even more committed to follow through. I just needed direction.

I started with an exercise from a book I randomly pulled off the bookshelf, the "Life Purpose Exercise" from one of Jack Canfield's books. Following his instructions, I listed my two unique personal qualities: dedication and desire.

Then I listed two ways I enjoy expressing these qualities with others: to help and to inspire. Plus, I described my perfect world: everyone living their best lives, aligned with their passions, exercising, eating well, and helping others—all while full of joy. Essentially, this vision was what I was seeking for myself.

Then I put these three ideas together: *My purpose is to use my dedication and desire to help and inspire others to live their best lives.*

Suddenly, it was clear to me! I knew what I was born to do!

The next morning, by six a.m., I had lost my new thread of clarity. Gone, just like that.

I just don't have a lot to contribute, I moaned. *Who will care about my story? I'm kidding myself. This is all a waste.*

To overcome my malaise, I decided to intentionally change my responses.

Change my response, and the outcome will be different, I repeated to myself.

First, I stopped visualizing the book as in the future, and started visualizing it in the now. I stopped and wrote, *I am writing.*

Before long, I stopped thinking, I was just doing. I was writing.

The affirmation came to me over and over throughout the days: *Change what I am doing today, and the results in the future will be different.*

This action renewed my confidence. The path might not be exactly clear to me—but I was going somewhere.

Doubt was malignant, however. It simply wouldn't let go. I lost the drive. I had no million-dollar idea. So, what was the point?

It got harder and harder to get out of bed. I struggled -- at work, at home, at the gym. Unmotivated. Definitely uninspired.

I saw this as weathering a storm but it was unending. I couldn't muster going to the gym. *What's the point?* I complained. Maybe swimming? A new workout machine? I kept trying to fight the despair.

Another week and I was re-inspired. I must have *something* to say that would help others?

I worked on my weight, my abs, my love handles—and I found that getting physical was stimulating. Then I put on a swimsuit—not a pretty sight!

I ordered P90X, a combination workout and diet program. I'd watched the commercial countless times. Though rigorous, the workout routines looked like fun. The DVDs gathered dust. Another new mantra gone by the wayside.

I decided to tell my mom about my writing a book and how I would travel around the world talking about it. She immediately told me she knew someone I should call. Moms are like that. One of her friends had recently started a coaching and motivational speaking business.

"He would be a great resource for you," she nudged.

"Sure, why not?"

"Great! Do you want to call him? Do you want his number? Should I call him for you?" She beamed.

"Okay, okay. Why don't you get me his phone number?"

"Really? I can do it for you," she offered.

"No, I will. I'll call."

This was certainly a change. Never before would I have called one of my mom's friends, especially not to ask for help, certainly not about trying to figure out what I wanted to do with my life. Motivational speaking? Well, I did think about it a lot. Maybe I should give it a try?

I sat with Todd's number for several days, before mustering the courage to make the call. My heart raced. "Hi, Todd. My mom gave me your number." I told him I was interested in motivational speaking, and he was full of suggestions, ideas, and questions.

"What have you done in this realm before?" he asked.

Realm? "I've been to several conferences, and I've done a lot of reading."

That was lame.

"So, you've been interested for a while now?"

"Yeah."

"I can help you move from being interested to committed. I'd love to be your coach."

"Great!"

My enthusiasm felt lame, but I did like the sound of having a coach. So what was a coach?

Todd offered to give a group of my friends a training on appreciation. I had no idea what he was going to do. However, this felt like a great first step.

After I hung up, I sat in silence. There was something about Todd's voice.

It was comforting. I felt like I could tell him anything.

The night of Todd's training, I had gathered all the women I could think of to invite. We met at Sophia's house. I came early, to meet Todd before the others arrived.

When Todd walked in and shook my hand, my heart beat fast. I looked into his eyes and he looked straight back into mine. He was fearless.

But I didn't feel the same connection I had on the phone. Also, he was older than I thought he would be. This was disappointing. Secretly I had hoped he was close to my own age. I had thought he might be a close friend.

Todd's class, however, was amazing. He did a wonderful job—and I was now convinced. Yes, I wanted to be a motivational speaker. I, too, wanted to help others in this way.

As I participated in Todd's group, I realized, *This could be me.* How would I do it differently? How would I lead such a group?

Then at the end of the class, I found myself making a commitment, to Todd, to the group, to myself. I would give a motivational talk by the end of May, two months from now.

Immediately I panicked and I fretted all the way home. How the hell would I do this? I wasn't a public speaker. What was I thinking? What would I say? Who would listen? Who would care? Crap!

But the words were out, and there was no going back.

Step one in preparing for my first ever motivational speech: Look the part.

OPTING IN

Fake it 'til you make it. To motivate myself, I needed to dress the part. I thought about Ellen DeGeneres. Her outfits rock. I could see myself wearing vests and jackets. My look.

That weekend, TJ went with me to the mall to find my power suit. He's a trooper that way.

I was totally playing out the *Pretty Woman* scene in my mind. TJ and I made our way to the women's department at Nordstrom and looked at some items on the rack. I had no idea what I was doing. Then a clerk came up and asked if she could help.

"Oh, can you ever!" I showed her my favorite Ellen suit on my iPhone and asked if there was any way we could get close to it.

"Sure, of course."

Could there be any other answer? And she was off. Sweet! This was the kind of sucking-up I was looking for.

A few minutes later, she was back with an armload. I could tell by the heap that I was going to like it. Many grays, blues, and blacks.

I started with the first gray suit and immediately ran into my first problem. My skin was pale, my butt had gotten huge, and this muffin top hung over the pants. *What!*

I sucked in as much as I could and tried on the size six. I had asked for a four; she had known the bad news before I did. Even the six had bulges in places there should not be bulges. This was really depressing.

The good news: the jacket fit perfectly. I looked awesome. The bad news: the jacket alone cost $1250. Panic!

49

What am I doing? I was trying on clothes that were clearly too small for a job I didn't even have. Shit, shit, shit. I was buying a power suit for a dream? I must be crazy.

I politely asked for a larger size.

"Oh, yes, these tend to run small."

"Sure they do."

After an hour or so, and many different suits, I had an outfit. A dark gray suit with a navy vest and a white-collared shirt underneath. I did look amazing. I could do anything in a suit like this, I affirmed to myself.

So another deep breath. "I'll take it."

But it scared the shit out of me. With chagrin, I said to TJ, "I guess I'm doing it."

He just grinned back. "I guess you are."

"This *is* my dream. Why is it so scary when it happens?"

Now to deal with my body. I'd really let go over the winter. At the job with Colin, I kept a chocolate drawer fully stocked. Now I was wearing a whole bag on my hips and my butt.

I increased going to the gym two days a week ... and gained weight! I hoped P90X would come in handy now.

The first phase of using the P90X program, you're supposed to eat a high percentage of protein. This had never been easy for me. I'm a carb girl. My thing is pasta, bread, and chips ... but now I had to commit to eggs, bacon, meats. But I would give it a try.

The worst part of P90X: taking the *before* photos. Pride-swallowing, gut-wrenching, humiliating. I put on my skimpiest bikini and stood against a white wall and let TJ take photos of me.

"You can go ahead and flex your arms," he said with a serious face.

"Thanks, dear, I am flexing."

"Oh, yeah, okay. I can see it now."

With my white skin that had not seen light all winter, my big butt, love handles, and muffin top—in the bikini photos, I wanted to run right out and buy more chocolate.

But I didn't. I finished week one. I even avoided the chocolate bowl at work *all* week.

Then TJ and I decided to go all out and buy the super-workout scale. It tells you how much you weigh and also breaks down your fat percentage, water weight, muscle weight, bone weight. Why had I thought this was a good idea?

We spent an hour messing around with the new scale and could hardly figure it out. This never happened to *me*. I have a gift for figuring out electronics *without* reading the directions. I can take any clock and change the time, no problem. This scale, however....We packaged it all back up and traded it in for one not so fancy, something more in our league.

I hopped on full of confidence—and I was at my highest weight in years! *Are you kidding me?*

All this work and I was gaining weight. From the couch, I stared at the new scale. I wanted to chuck it out the door.

TJ yelled from the kitchen, "Hey, do you want a piece of chocolate for dessert?"

I dragged myself off the couch and crawled into bed with all my clothes on.

I woke the next morning to my ever-so-cute husband who gently said, "Love, you need to stop playing the victim."

Okay, deep breath. This was a new day.

CHAPTER 5
My Shame

"I would rather shed a million tears over the ugly truth than smile over a million beautiful lies." - Unknown

Going for your dreams is a bumpy road. I kept pushing myself out of my comfort zone.

Todd's help to get my motivational speaking off the ground came in the shape of a check for $3750. That seemed a lot for a tryout. However, this *was* my dream. Right?

I did believe—deep down—that motivational speaking would lead to something greater than my life had been up until now. I would have a real sense of purpose. My life would have meaning, maybe for the first time.

In the initial training class with Todd and my friends, he had asked if U2's song "I Still Haven't Found What I'm Looking For" resonated with anyone. I was the only one to raise my hand. This song didn't just resonate with me. It *was* me! I knew I hadn't found what I was looking for, but at least I was looking!

I had read tons of self-help books, tried different jobs, gone back to school. Nothing had turned on the light.

Throughout my searching, however, two things had remained constant: I found that I enjoyed improving myself ... and that I loved to write. During the countless hours of reading about motivation, success, and passions, I realized I was no longer trying to motivate myself. I actually enjoyed the material. It was fun.

As I struggled to uncover a clearer picture of what I wanted to do with my life, an answer began to take shape. I was quite familiar with feeling lost and alone. This had been my journey. This was it! I would help others who also felt lost and alone.

For the first time, I knew. This was what I wanted to do ... and I wanted to be at the front of the room.

After this revelation, every time I went to a conference for my job or attended a seminar, I envisioned myself leading the program. I could re-member back to every assembly in school when I was a kid. I remembered them with such clarity. How had I forgotten that I knew then what I wanted? I had always wanted to be the one presenting. Maybe I wasn't ready before, but now I was.

My first assignment from Todd was to come up with twenty stories of the good, the bad, and the ugly of Molly. These stories would help me to craft my motivational speech for May. I quickly came up with many more than twenty. I had more stories in me than I realized.

Now the fun part, crafting a speech. It started with defining what made me unique. What special advantage did I have? Why did I desire to be extraordinary?

My advantage: I knew how it felt to be confused, to feel hurt, even to feel alone when not alone. This technique helped me to focus, and it felt really good to get myself and my life organized.

OPTING IN

My first story would be five minutes. I had witnessed the death of a friend. I was nervous to tell it. I hadn't talked about that night in a long time. Did I really want to?

My first audience was one, Todd, over the phone. My stomach was in knots as I dialed his number.

Nervous, I kept adding details and the story kept growing. On top of that, at this exact time my black lab Lucy wanted my attention. She kept nudging me, and I would forget where I was in the story and add another detail.

Todd made several comments and I felt like shit. He didn't think it was the best story to lead with. I tried to suck it up.

Skip ahead one week. If I thought I was nervous the last time, it paled in comparison to this second call, even though I was ultra-prepared. I had practiced three separate openings for the speech in the shower, in the car, to TJ, to my dog.

Then when I called, Todd wasn't ready.

"Call me back in fifteen minutes," he said.

"Sure, no problem." *Shit, now I have to psych myself up all over again?*

I pumped myself up with the music "Free Falling" by Tom Petty. I needed some music with a strong beat and a fast rhythm to pump me up to deliver my stories. Then I called twenty minutes later so I wouldn't seem too eager.

First, Todd asked me about the venue I had selected for my talk. I excitedly told him I had found the perfect place. It was halfway between two groups of friends, so they could all come.

Fixed:

"As your coach, I'm telling you, no."

Oh?

He explained that I should have *two* talks and make them closer for people to come.

Okay, so my perfect setting was out, meaning one of my stories was out. I sucked up my pride and gave him my power-suit story.

"Okay, I like the energy," he said. "I have some comments, but let's hear the other one."

Not the response I was looking for, but I braved it and told him my "Free Falling" story about psyching myself up by singing very loudly in the car.

"Well, I'm not sure we've found it yet," he said.

Are you kidding me? All three stories rejected? Talk one, crash and burn. Talk two, crash and burn. Talk three, crash and burn. I couldn't hold back my tears.

"So, tell me, where you are right now with this?" he asked.

"I'm feeling disappointed," I squeaked out, coughing to cover up my voice cracking.

Such a wimp! I chastised myself. I was so pathetic. Here I was bawling on the phone to a guy I'd just met because he didn't like my ideas.

Suck it up, Molly. Hang in there, Ellen. I'll make it to your show before you retire or die of old age, I promise.

Todd tried to boost me back up. "You won't be perfect at this yet. You've only been at it for two weeks."

That was true.

He then raved about my courage and fearlessness. I half believed him.

Then when I thought about it later, Todd's criticisms were exactly what I'd needed. If he hadn't pushed me after the first story, I wouldn't have come up with the other three. Who knows what I might do next? My second batch was much better than the first. If I kept getting better each time, my first five minutes would blow everyone away! I was curious to find out what I had in me, and I was willing to peel back the layers.

The next week, I took a day off work and drove an hour and a half north to Steamboat Springs to meet Todd. To be honest, I very much dreaded the meeting. The two phone sessions had been grueling and I wasn't looking forward to another meltdown.

I made it to his house in record time. It was a beautiful spring day, and the roads were clear, no snow. As fearful as I was about the meeting, I enjoyed the drive. However, as I pulled into his driveway at the edge of town, my hands began to sweat and my heart raced.

Todd opened the door and, in a panic about what to say, I asked if I could use his bathroom.

Then, sitting at his kitchen table, on my laptop I showed him the PowerPoint presentation I was building. I felt good about it and figured it needed only fine-tuning.

He had me stand and tell each of my stories as I showed each slide. I mustered animation and inflection. I was way past my comfort zone.

As I talked, I could tell Todd wanted something more from me. Even I knew my PowerPoint talk was full of fluff—wishing, hoping, and dreaming. It was a feel-good talk and Todd wasn't buying it.

"Tell me what you're avoiding, Molly. The raw, ugly, vulnerable truth. The part of you that you don't want anyone to see, the shame."

I swallowed, and looked down. I had been avoiding my real story: the death of my brother. I hadn't mentioned it to Todd, but he knew it from my mom.

The loss and trauma were still very raw for me. I didn't want to go there. I didn't want anyone to see this dark part of me.

Todd kept talking about *process* goals versus *outcome* goals. He explained how my talk, for now, was an *outcome* goal, that I was focused on the end result. That was true. I had committed to giving a motivational speech the end of May. I couldn't think about anything else. I had to get it right.

Todd explained how outcome goals tend to lead to upset. He used weight loss as an example. If I had a goal of losing twenty pounds by a certain date, and I lost only fifteen pounds by that date, would that be a failure? As an *outcome* goal, yes. As a *process* goal, no; losing fifteen pounds would be a tremendous achievement.

This made sense to me. I could certainly relate to weight loss. How did he know?

Anyway, I had been trying to create a perfect speech. When, in reality, creating a speech is about the *process* and insights gained along the way. Ah-ha! My stories needed to be the truth, the gut-wrenching truth. That is what moves people, he told me.

I stopped the slide show. The story of my brother was surfacing. Memories had been drifting up over the last week, and I'd been shoving them back down. I wasn't proud of the story. I didn't want to think about it. I didn't want to remember. I certainly didn't want to share it.

I took a deep breath and said, "This isn't pretty." Todd nodded in response. I sat. I couldn't do this standing up.

"My older brother, Ben, was one of those kids who always got into trouble," I said. "Whatever he did wrong, he got busted. On top of that, he was diabetic, and he experimented with drugs and alcohol and ended up in rehab. He needed a lot of attention. He taxed my parents, consumed them.

"I just wanted everyone to be happy," I continued. "So, for the most part, I did what I was told. I stayed out of trouble and tried to be easy for my parents. This worked most of the time.

"Then one week I'd just had enough. Ben had a diabetic reaction while driving and dented the front end of his truck. I don't know if it scared me, or I'd just had enough, but I snapped. When he asked me to take him to town to get his truck fixed, I said no.

"'I've had enough!' I yelled at him. 'Everything's always about you! I'm sick of it! Find someone else to take your truck. I'm not doing it.'

"I went to bed mad and didn't talk to Ben the next morning. In fact, I got up early so I could take the bus and wouldn't have to ride with him. Later in the day, I ran into him at school. He looked over at me as if he wanted to say something, but I didn't give him the chance. I turned my back and walked away."

I sighed, embarrassed to look Todd in the eyes. "That was the last time I ever saw Ben. He died in a car accident that afternoon."

I saw the tears in Todd's eyes, and held back my own.

Quietly, I said, "It took me years to realize Ben's accident wasn't my fault. I do believe everything happens for a reason and that it was his time. I know it wasn't my fault. But I've lived with the pain of our last conversation since the day he died."

I sighed heavily. "I didn't get a chance to make it right. If I could have just one more talk, one more conversation. But it was too late. He was gone."

The old familiar regret and shame filled me. I hated this story. I bent over and cried. "I still miss him! I wish I could do it over."

Todd put his hand on my back. "It's not too late to have that conversation, Molly."

I sighed. "I didn't realize how badly I needed to say I'm sorry. It's been weighing on me."

"Your brother doesn't need to hear it, Molly. You do. You don't need to carry this anymore."

With tears in my eyes, I looked at Todd, feeling forlorn. "That last look he gave me at school, he was okay with me telling him *no*."

Todd nodded and, for the first time since Ben's death, I felt lighter. Then I laughed at myself. "I've spent a lifetime of saying *yes* to people, because the one time I said *no* it didn't work out so well." I shook my head. "I didn't feel I deserved any better."

In this moment, I started to see why my *good* life hadn't resonated with me. I wasn't living for myself. I wasn't living my dream. I didn't even know what my dream was. I had lived most of my life for all the wrong reasons, a life of saying yes. I was ready to live for me and let the rest go.

Todd smiled. "You can let it go."

I nodded. "I get it now." I felt a self-love I'd never had.

"You've been through a lot," Todd said, "and you are courageous."

"I am, aren't I?" Wow. This was the real me. "I'm done with living from fear."

Todd left me alone to craft a goodbye letter to my brother.

> Ben,
>
> I am so sorry. I've been trying to tell you that for twenty years. I've been saying it over and over, through my actions, my life, but never through my words.
>
> I didn't know two things: that you didn't need to hear it, and that I needed to say it.
>
> My last words to you, Ben, were in anger. I don't know if I was jealous of your time with our parents, or scared that I could lose you. I so clearly remember that last look you gave me, one of love and forgiveness; and I turned away and left you with a look of anger. I could never forgive myself for that before.
>
> Your life was so short, Ben. You should have had everything you wanted. You should have had a sister who left you with love. I'm sorry.
>
> Today, I do know and remember that I have always loved you. I now know you have always been with me, gently showing me the way. Brother, I hear you.
>
> I have laid down the weight. In honor of you, and me, I will be true to myself now and find my way. I know you are with me and that I am not alone. Now I see the possibilities and I am excited

about my life. You have made me strong. Thank you for being my big brother.

I love you.

~ ~ ~

My high on life's possibilities didn't last long. God's gift? What gift? How on earth would I ever make a difference?

Then it came to me, again. I knew what it was like to feel like a victim ... and I was beginning to get an inkling of how not to be one. They say to teach what you know. I was learning how to be my real self: courageous, smart, and lovable.

After my trip to Steamboat, TJ and I spent a week in Moab, Utah, where my brother Lee and his family were visiting from New Hampshire. My family owned a house outside of town and we all met up there once a year to mountain bike, hike, and enjoy the desert. While in Moab, I spent a lot of time thinking about my conversation with Todd about my brother Ben. Todd had told me that without this old weight I would now see all kinds of possibilities for my life. But I didn't. Why not? Why did I still feel so ashamed?

I pondered all these thoughts over the week. Oddly, while Lee went mountain biking with friends, I felt suspended. I didn't want to participate. I worried. Was my realization with Todd enough? I had wasted so much valuable time. Why wasn't life revealing itself to me?

Then, realizing I was causing my own suffering, I knew I couldn't just sit around and wait for life to show up. So, I invited Lee, TJ, and the rest of the family to dinner. Lee was immediately available and psyched. They all were. It was as simple as that. I had just stumbled onto the secret of life: Take action.

Even so, after this revelation, it took an extraordinary effort to keep myself motivated and to fight my own resistance to myself. My old ways kept dragging on me, refusing to let go, deeply ingrained.

I will not give in!

CHAPTER 6
My Even Darker Secret

"We can only appreciate the miracle of a sunrise if we have
waited in the darkness." - Unknown

I was sinking. Despite my pep talk to myself, I couldn't shake a dark feeling.

What had Todd done to me? Why had he pushed me so hard? I couldn't do this. I wasn't brave enough.

Lying on the couch, curled up in a ball, I gasped. *I don't want to share my sad stories! You were supposed to guide me! I shouldn't have rushed into this. I shouldn't have let you in. I shouldn't have trusted you. I am so naïve!*

I ached for my long-lost joy, innocence, laughter, fun. It was gone. It was all gone. I had buried it! Why had Todd made me drag it out again? I felt worse than ever.

Sharing my story of my brother was supposed to help. I was supposed to feel free and full of possibility. Why did I feel even worse? The part of me that I had hidden was growing, not disappearing! I had failed as a human being. My shame had gone from an occasional whisper to a deafening roar.

Night after night, I agonized ... and poured out my rage, disappointment, disgust, and fear in crying fits that lasted hours. I was paralyzed by a deepest despair, gripped by a fury and unable to function.

In these dark moments, a memory crept in, another regret I had shoved down. Very deep.

No way was I telling this one! No way.

However, as the days went on, I realized I couldn't avoid telling Todd *this* story. I couldn't *not* tell it. That really sucked!

On our next call, I told him how out of control this all made me feel.

"You can go through this, Molly, and come out the other side. Or you can stay where you are and not change, not transform. It's a choice, Molly. You choose."

I nodded. I knew he was right. I really did want to heal and transform. I knew I had to tell Todd my even darker secret. We agreed that he would come to my house.

I held on for five days and nights while TJ and I moved. We rented Sophia's house. For the winter, she and her husband went to South Carolina to be closer to family. TJ and I had agreed that my days of commuting and living apart were over for us. It had taken a toll on our marriage and we both wanted things to work between us. Sophia and her husband left most of the furniture, so our move in was quick and easy. I moved what little I had from my apartment, TJ sealed up our trailer, and we put our things in storage in Moab, Utah. TJ talked to his boss and was allowed to do most of his work from home. Everything was falling into place.

Then while TJ windsurfed at South Padre Island, Texas for two weeks, I let the memories of my dark secret come. The pain, shame, hurt, and regret all hit me. I had been numb. Now I was feeling it all.

Then on that Saturday morning, Todd walked through the door. As soon as I saw him, my worry eased. My suffering was almost over. This was a cancer slowly killing me and it was time to get it out.

I paused. "I'm about to share my darkest secret. Can I trust you?"

He nodded. "Molly, of course you can. I'm here for you. I'm not going anywhere."

I nodded and began. "It was my college days. I had some incredible friends and I'd just discovered alcohol. The freedom I found in booze amazed me. I could be free for a night. Sweet freedom from the pain of losing my brother Ben. I found comfort in numbing out. I would study hard all week without drinking, then on the weekend go all out. I followed the booze. I loved the feeling of losing myself. It felt like time out from my life."

Todd just listened, and I felt he *heard* me.

"We were at a fraternity rugby party. I had recently started playing rugby and, for the first time, I felt like I belonged. I'd been invited to this party that was a huge deal. Rugby was the *it* sport. To be invited meant I had done something right, finally.

"As soon as my girlfriends and I made it through the door, the beer never stopped. We were all a bit overwhelmed. We had walked past this house many times. Now, we were here.

"It all happened so fast. We were lined up against a wall in the living room, working our way toward a good buzz. No one was talking. We were just drinking and watching, in awe.

"Then a group of guys walked in and we all took notice. It was obvious they weren't students there. I overheard that they were from a military school. That made sense, because they were ripped. They were like gods to us freshmen.

"One of the guys headed in my direction. I immediately looked away. He got close and my heart raced. This was my chance to finally be one of the cool kids, and I couldn't even say a word. But he started talking to me, like he was interested. Me? In this huge room full of attractive women?

"He shared his drink with me and kept talking. Then he asked if I wanted to go for a walk. I did the only thing I could think to do. I turned to my girlfriends for the answer. 'Molly, go! Yes, go.' They were so psyched for me. They all had huge grins on their faces."

I looked up at Todd, feeling clenched. I'd been staring into my lap.

"You're doing great," he encouraged.

I nodded and immersed back into the memory. "We walked outside and I was immediately cold. I didn't have a jacket, but I played it cool and I didn't say anything. Suddenly, I started to get a really bad feeling. I wanted to go back inside, but I was too scared to speak up. Before I realized it, we were in the woods ... and he started kissing me."

I paused and grimaced, remembering. I stared into my lap. "This was the first time I had done anything more than kiss a guy on the lips ... and his tongue was all over my mouth. I had always thought my first real kiss would be amazing, something special. But this was forced, very forced. Rough, too rough. I wanted him to stop, but his hands were all over me. I froze, thinking *no, no, no.* But I couldn't speak. I didn't know what to do. I didn't know how to make him stop. I couldn't make a sound.

"So I shut down. I did nothing. I was on my back ... and the ground hurt, digging into my back. I focused on the pain, how sharp it was. I was so cold, and the earth was so hard on my bare skin.

"No! No! No! This isn't happening! This can't be happening!

"Then in one sharp movement, he was inside me, ripping, many times, so many times. I thought it would never end."

I sighed heavily. I still couldn't look up at Todd. "I was so ashamed," I whispered. "I'd never had sex before. It was supposed to be special. It wasn't."

I caught my breath. Todd waited patiently. His patience wrapped me like a warm blanket.

"When he stopped," I continued quietly, "I couldn't move. I couldn't believe what had just happened. He put my clothes back on me and pulled me up from the ground. I had dirt and twigs in my hair. He grabbed my arm hard and stared hard at me. 'You will never talk about this to anyone.' I nodded, shivering, disheveled."

I could barely breathe as I finished the story. "I didn't even know his name. Was I raped? I didn't know. Was this my fault? It must have been my fault. I had walked into the woods with him; I drank his beer, had sex. I hated myself. I had let it happen. I was mortified.

"I went back to my dorm room. I crawled into my bed in a ball. I didn't cry. I was numb, cold and numb.

"I opened my eyes and saw my floor advisor, Winston, a huge guy. He was my angel. He picked me up and carried me to the hospital. He didn't ask what had happened. He knew.

"At the hospital, they wanted to do a rape kit. I refused. So many people were staring at me. I felt so violated. Winston watched over me at the hospital, my angel. He was my voice when I didn't have one.

"They gave me something, and I felt so tired. The pain went away, and I was out. I woke up in my dorm bed, and Winston was watching over me.

69

"The next time I got out of bed it was Tuesday. The first thing I did was fail two exams. I was so out of it that I couldn't even read them. My eyes would stick on the end of a sentence, and I couldn't make them go to the next line. I had to meet with the dean or governing board. I almost got kicked out of college. I asked for a second chance. Grades were all I had. If I failed at college, I would have nothing."

I stopped here. I had not told Todd the whole story. I had left out many parts. It was hard enough to voice this much. I had never told anyone.

I hunched over and cried into my hands. I didn't want Todd to see my shame. I curled into a ball. I wanted to disappear. I was so cold.

Todd touched my back, and I felt safe. I asked if he would sit next to me on the couch.

"Of course. Of course I will."

He sat next to me. I pulled up my feet and curled into a ball. He held me and I cried—for my innocence lost, for how much I hated myself, how ashamed I was.

I went in and out. One moment, I panicked and looked around. Todd gave me a Kleenex and I reminded myself to be brave.

"Why are you holding on to this memory?" he asked. "What are you getting from it?"

"Getting from it?"

"You can sit here all day and cry, but you'll still be stuck," Todd said. "Release this and be big, Molly. It's keeping you small. You need to get over yourself and release this."

"Get over myself?" I started crying. "How can I get over myself? I don't get it."

Todd held me, and I felt so close to him, so connected. For a long time we sat in silence.

After a while he said, "You look better."

I felt better, and I nodded. "It's time to get over myself."

CHAPTER 7
Going Beyond My Fear

"Well done is better than well said." - Benjamin Franklin

After Todd left, I went for a walk in the meadow above my house. The air was crisp and I welcomed the cold on my face.

I was in awe of what had just happened. I'd had the courage to tell the story of who I really am, with my whole heart. For the first time I didn't skip over the part of me that I hated. I had allowed Todd to see me, all of me.

With that excruciating vulnerability, something magical had happened, a connection, a connection I hadn't known or I had forgotten.

I had lived my whole life in shame, the shame of saying no to my brother, the shame of throwing away my virginity. To hide these feelings from the world, I had disappeared, disconnected, lonely but safe.

Now I was free, free from being invisible. Todd had seen me. He knew me.

As I continued to walk through the mountain meadow, I felt reborn, full of such joy, feeling connected. I felt like I could do anything! Be anything. The possibilities for my life were endless! I was really living *my* life.

I wanted to live! I embraced the moment. "I'm alive!" I shouted with exuberance.

When I got back from the walk, still on an amazing high, I sent Todd an e-mail.

> Todd, wow. I *am* in awe of our time together. I know there is a reason you came into my life. All my life has been a desperate journey, not knowing who I am, not finding answers, anywhere, with anyone.
>
> I have to confess, in December I'd given up. I was so tired. I just wanted to quit. I almost did. I was going to kill myself.
>
> But then I didn't. I had an idea. I would write a book. It would change my life. I would travel. I would lecture. Then my mom told me about you.
>
> Todd, I think my soul connected with you. My soul saw a light and led me to you. There was even something about you over the phone, your voice.
>
> I'm laughing at myself now. You said, "You need to get over yourself." You're right. But I don't even know where to begin.
>
> So I am taking a deep breath and letting go. Thank you.

I felt closer to Todd now. He got me. No one ever had before, and I could feel it: I would never be the same.

I was tired of waiting for my life to start. I was on fire, ready to take it all on!

What did I want my life to look like? I wanted to conquer my fear and everything I had been afraid of. I was tired of playing it safe. I was ready to play full out, to go big.

OPTING IN

As I thought about all my fears, one big one began to surface, then quickly rose to the top: telling my dad I loved him. I couldn't remember the last time I had said those words to him. I think more than anyone else, I had been hiding from my dad. I didn't want him to see my shame. I didn't want to disappoint him. Now I realized I desperately missed him.

I waited until the next morning, stalling. I stared at my cell phone, my heart racing. My finger hovered over the call button. Several times, I set the phone down, then picked it up again.

Just do it, I finally told myself and I punched his number, part of me hoping for voicemail.

He answered. I was glad he did, but I worried that he could hear my heart beating through the phone.

We started *our* conversation, the one we always had; the one about work, weather, running.

Then he said, "So, what are you up to today?"

This was it. No more stalling. It was time.

I took a deep breath and told him there was something I needed to tell him. I could tell he was nervous on the other end for what might be coming. I told him what I had wanted to say for years. "I love you, Dad."

There was silence on the other end. I could tell he was choked up.

After a period of silence, he said, "You have no idea how long and how badly I've needed to hear that."

Now, I got choked up.

Seven or eight times during that conversation, he told me he loved me, too. He said, "One day you just stop saying it, and you never know if your kids still want to hear it."

I said, "The answer is always yes, Dad. We do want to hear it."

This was one of the greatest conversations I ever had with my dad. He opened up to me about his dreams and the last conversation he'd had with his father, stories we had never shared.

That door had been closed a very long time. Never again would I hesitate to tell my dad that I love him, that I really love him.

With this call, all pain, suffering, and expectations I'd had about my dad were gone. I got my dad back that morning.

I was on such a high after this call. Everything was so clear. I'd never felt so much love, love for myself, love for everyone. I was in love with being alive. I wanted more.

I wanted to *coach*, like Todd. This surprised me. I had grown.

I was terrified. But I would go beyond my fear. It was time to go beyond myself, to help others. No more stalling.

I had coffee with Todd the next weekend. He was in town for his daughter's soccer game. I had so much I wanted to tell him. It felt like I had lived a lifetime in this last week.

I beamed. "I want to coach."

"Of course," he simply said.

I was looking for more of a response than that and I just stared at him.

"It's a perfect fit for you, Molly. You're a natural. I know you can really help people."

My huge self-doubt cropped up. "I don't feel ready. I don't have any training."

"Take the Landmark Forum."

That was all I needed to hear. I had no idea what the Landmark Forum was, but I was taking it! Now!

As soon as I got home, I went online and Googled *Landmark*. This worldwide company offered innovative programs for living an extraordinary life.

Yes, I need to do this!

The flagship program was three days and an evening, from Friday morning to Sunday night, then completing on a Tuesday night.

Perfect! I could do it over the weekend. This weekend!

My eyes raced across the computer screen, looking for dates in Denver. Crap. Nothing soon enough. Where else? Tucson!

I booked Tucson, Arizona. That Friday.

From the moment I stepped into the conference room at the Hotel Arizona, I didn't know what to expect. The weekend is now a blur. We started at seven a.m. and went until ten at night. Most of the time, we talked about completing the past, cleaning up incomplete areas in our lives, and bringing about our transformation. People went to the front of the room and shared stories of their agonizing memories. The facilitator then coached us on what that experience meant to us.

When I stood, I talked about being my authentic self and finding areas in my life where I wasn't being authentic. The facilitator, Will, asked what event had happened to me. I remembered someone telling me I was shy, and my mom telling others I was shy. So, I had come to believe I *was* shy and should not be outgoing.

I laughed now. "I'm *not* shy. That wasn't real. It's never been real. I *can* be a motivational speaker!" Everyone applauded.

At the break, many people came up to me and thanked me for sharing. "You got up there. You're not shy," they said.

I grinned. "Yeah, I see that now."

I was on fire. *My* story had touched, moved, and inspired others. I had touched their lives. *I* had done that.

During another break, I called Todd and excitedly told him I was taking the Landmark Forum in Tucson.

"You're kidding! No way." He was so excited for me.

Filled with exuberance from the workshop, I said, "Todd, there's actually something I want to clean up with you."

"Great, go for it."

"I've been thinking about you a lot. I feel a deep connection to you. Opening up to you created a bond ... and I think I love you ... and I've been feeling wrong for feeling that way."

Todd immediately asked about the other parts of the course. I was surprised that I didn't need his direct response. I felt clear. Just telling him had given me clarity.

A few minutes later, he said, "Sorry, I wasn't able to talk to you freely before. I can talk now. Molly, I love you, too. I feel the same way, and you're right. Of course it isn't wrong. It is absolutely not wrong."

I was excited that Todd told me he loved me. I was special to him.

I felt so free! I was excited to have this connection with him. I felt gotten.

CHAPTER 8
Once Again, a Quitter

"How lucky I am to have something that makes saying goodbye
so hard." - Carol Sobieski and Thomas Meehan, *Annie*

My first public speech was only days away. I had invited friends, co-workers and colleagues, anyone I could think of. I had committed.

Now, I worried. Though I had practiced my talk with TJ several times, what if I forgot what to say or I stumbled over my words, or I talked too fast and rushed through the material? What if everyone just sat there and stared at me?

I had avoided sharing my speech with Todd. I would run through it with him before I gave it to the audience.

TJ and I decided to spend this weekend with friends, before the talk, in Moab, Utah. The trip took us three and half hours. We enjoyed the hot dry air of the desert.

However, in the back of my mind, never far from my thoughts, was my speech. I talked with Todd Saturday and decided to drive from Moab to Steamboat on Sunday, to practice the speech with him. TJ and I would leave our visit a day early.

We woke early on Sunday and played tennis with our friends. The game ran long, so we had to hurry through coffee and breakfast. Our friends ate and talked while we packed and reloaded the van.

TJ and I had never driven from Moab to Steamboat and I was unsure how long it would take. He seemed to know the exact distance. However, neither of us was even close in judging how long the trip would take. We were still over an hour away when Todd texted me, asking where I was.

I could tell he was bothered that I was late. He had to organize rides for his kids. I wanted to skip the whole thing, turn around and go home. I had rushed him, and myself.

"It'll work out," he said. "It'll be fine."

I felt like shit, and TJ was driving so fast.

Even so, I managed to be okay with all of this. My silence was freaking TJ out, though. He was waiting for me to lose it. Strangely, I didn't.

"Oh, shit," I then blurted.

He looked over, expecting my meltdown. "Do you want to turn around? We can. Molly, you don't have to do this. We can turn around and forget the whole thing."

"No, that's okay. I just remembered that my bidding deadline is in a few minutes for my eBay items."

"What?"

I had bid on several very expensive diaper bags for two pregnant employees in the office, to give them at a baby shower. I had strategized that if I bid on several, I was sure to win the two I needed. I had already won one. I needed just one more bag. I got out my iPhone.

Meanwhile, the van was flying all over the road. Poor Lucy in the back had all of her nails out, holding on for dear life as she slid from side to side.

I upped my eBay bid. The minutes ticked down.

"Yes!" I screamed. I had won! Now, I just needed to be *outbid* on my backup third bid. I wanted only two bags.

As we entered Todd's neighborhood, I was staring at my iPhone. I could *not* win a third bag! I currently had the highest bid and prayed that someone else would bid just higher.

Four minutes to go. In Todd's driveway, I jumped out of the van, staring at my iPhone. I waved TJ away without looking at him. He backed out of the driveway, to go find a place to walk Lucy. Watching the minutes tick down on eBay, I knocked on Todd's door.

When he opened it, I blurted, "Can I use your bathroom?" I needed to buy a few minutes to finish my eBay negotiation.

Then in the bathroom, my phone didn't work. So, I stood in Todd's kitchen, watching the eBay screen. One minute left.

Suddenly, I remembered where I was and Todd was staring at me quizzically. I had totally forgotten about my talk. I looked at my iPhone. I had just won the third bag. Crap.

"Ready to start?" Todd asked.

I just stood there staring at him. I hadn't thought about my talk the entire trip over. I couldn't think of one thing to say, so I stalled. "I just need a minute."

I blanked, and he stared at me. With a lump in my throat, I choked out a few words. Then I found my groove, the story: about living the life we love and what keeps us falling short. I relayed the last words I had spoken to my brother Ben and the weight I had been carrying. I talked about my journey of guilt—

Todd's phone rang, his kids ready to be picked up. I rushed the end of my talk, feeling like a total shit.

I didn't want Todd to know that his phone call made me feel I wasn't important, that what I had to say wasn't important, that he had put me on the sideline. I wanted to run.

He needed to go, but he just sat there. He mentioned a few things I could do differently to improve my delivery. I don't remember what he said. My mind was already in the van headed out of town.

Then Todd said very clearly, "You need to really get in there and mine the gold, Molly. Really get present to how it felt to hold on to that as your truth. For twenty years, you held that as your truth, Molly. Really put it out there now."

Oh.

That's when I got it. That was when I understood the magnitude of the weight I had been carrying over Ben's death and its impact in my life. As Todd repeated the twenty years of blaming myself, it sunk in and hit me hard. I swallowed, blinked, trying to keep tears at bay.

Then I did what I always do. I shut down. Completely. This was too much, way too much. I got up and looked for a trashcan. "I need to go."

"Is something wrong? You seem upset."

"No, I'm good. I need to go."

"What happened? Did I say too much? Did I throw too much at you? Did I freak you out?"

"No, I'm good."

Where was his fucking trashcan! Under the sink? No. Next to the bathroom? No. Did he not have a fucking trashcan? *Fuck. Get me out of here!*

"Molly, come on, talk to me. What did I say? What's showing up for you?"

To the concern in Todd's voice, I answered, "I'm good. Where is your trashcan?"

"Here, just give it to me."

I handed him the Kleenex I had shredded while dabbing at my tears. I headed for the door. "I have to go."

"Molly..."

"I'm good," I said. I had my hand on the doorknob and looked back to say goodbye.

Todd held his arms out and I wanted so badly to hug him. I wanted him to wrap his arms around me and hold me. I wanted him to make me feel safe. Instead, I turned and walked out the door.

He followed me. "Molly..."

Halfway down his driveway, I turned. "I can't. I just can't. I can't do this."

I ran down the driveway to the van where TJ was waiting. I jumped in, and TJ and Lucy both looked at me, puzzled.

"Please get me out of here," I said.

As we drove home from Steamboat, my resistance turned to anger—toward Todd. He had pushed me. Why did he have to probe when he didn't have time to hear the answer?

What were these feelings surfacing? I pushed them back down. I couldn't risk these feelings.

How could I possibly give my talk now? *Great, really great. If this is coaching, you can have it. I'm done.*

I fell asleep in the van as TJ drove us home. I slept hard for over an hour, a deep sleep. When I woke, the anger was gone. Somehow, a peace had come over me.

Now I realized I had struggled with my practice talks because I had been holding back. Anytime I had felt emotions surfacing, I had shoved them down. If I were brave, I would let myself feel. I took a deep breath.

At home, I called Todd to apologize.

"You don't have to be sorry," he said.

He knew exactly what was going on with me. In sharing my story of being raped, in addition to my guilt over my brother's death, I had glimpsed what bottling up these experiences had done to my life. At my core, I had believed I was trash, that I deserved what had happened to me. As a human being, I had failed. I was worthless, completely unlovable.

When Todd reminded me that I'd been holding this for twenty years, emotion had rushed in. I had lived numb for so many years.

Then I had instantly wanted to quit the coaching with Todd, one of my lifelong patterns. Whenever I got scared, confused, or uncertain, I ran away.

Was I still running? Couldn't I shake this?

I can stay in the confusion, I can stay small, or....

~ ~ ~

It was less than an hour until I was to give my first talk. I had booked a room at a local library. I arrived early to set up and arrange chairs. My mom and TJ would be here. Colin would be here. Would Todd come?

There was no preparing myself, though. I was terrified. What if no one else showed up? What if they did? What if it made no difference?

TJ was amazing. He set up cameras, made sure that I had water, and gave the room a final look. I headed to the bathroom for a final check in the mirror. Wearing my Ellen DeGeneres power suit helped.

"You did it, girl," I said to myself in the mirror. "You're here. You're doing it."

I took a deep breath and walked back into the room. Todd walked in, and my heart raced. He gave me a hug, offered words of encouragement, and went to find a seat.

Then it was just me—in front of the room. I told the story of seeing my brother Ben for the last time. The old emotions rushed through my body. The loss, the hurt, the sorrow, and I let the tears come. My voice cracked, but it was okay.

I looked around the room. Tears filled their eyes, too.

I was free of my past! The years were suddenly gone. The weight was lifted.

TJ and I went on a much-needed vacation. We dropped off our pup with my dad and flew to the Caribbean, at St. Lucia. Ten days of beach, sunshine, scuba diving, relaxing, and afternoon cocktails. It was a nice break.

As I relaxed, my mind wandered back to my talk, how it had gone, ultimately to Todd. Why had he left so quickly? When would I see him again? What had everyone thought about what I said?

Back home, Todd and I exchanged texts, e-mails, and voice mails—a serious game of phone tag. We kept failing to connect.

I constantly checked my phone. Why couldn't I reach him? Had I done something wrong? Was he mad at me? Didn't he care?

I replayed our last conversation in my mind, at his house, *before* my talk. Over and over.

I woke at two a.m., checked my phone. Nothing.

I tried *not* to obsess. I tried to laugh about it. I would reach him and we would laugh at all of this.

At the end of two days, I sent an e-mail. I cried as I typed. I must say goodbye.

> Todd, I cannot connect with you. I'm confused. I'm not angry. What I learned from you about myself is amazing. My life will forever be different because of you. That is what I will remember. Todd, I care about you more than you know, but I am hurting. I

don't want there to be hard feelings, but it's time to go my own way. Goodbye. Molly

He replied very early the next morning.

Hi, Molly, thank you for your honesty. I love the stand you are making for your happiness. Should your perspective change, please know I will be available with open arms and an open heart. Thanks for all you have given me and taught me. I care about you deeply. Todd

I felt like shit on so many levels. Yesterday, I'd spent all day on the couch, then drunk myself into a stupor at a wedding with a good friend. For the longest time, I had chatted with an Australian man sitting on the bar stool next to me; he looked a lot like Mel Gibson. We talked about travel, differences in our countries, just about everything in between. Then he leaned over and kissed me.

What the fuck? I didn't even know this man. Then I kissed him.

I am not this person! I berated myself. *This is not who I am.*

I didn't tell TJ. I didn't want to hurt him. I thought I should tell him, though. I didn't want any secrets between us. However, I wasn't brave enough.

I wasn't brave.

I am so average, so ordinary.

Is that a bad thing? I argued with myself. *Why is it so hard for me to be happy?*

Why did I dislike myself? Why did I need to be extraordinary? Why did I never finish things?

I needed to get back on track. I hadn't been working out, and I'd put the weight back on. So much for my ninety-day program.

I'd start again on Monday. I was lying. I dreaded the workouts.

I also missed Todd. Had I done the right thing? I didn't even finish my three months with him. I'd just quit. I missed our talks. I missed his help. I could certainly use his help right now.

I had started this motivational speaking thing, but where was I going with it? Nowhere.

Once again, at the bottom. *Do something, anything,* I chastised myself.

Depression, out of here! I commanded.

So, I did the mother of all P90X workouts, plyometrics, jump training, and I started feeling human again.

I was working my way back up. I realized I could forgive myself for my constant ups and downs. I even told TJ what had happened at the wedding ... and I realized I *did* love him.

CHAPTER 9
Breaking My Old Pattern

"Be who you are and say what you feel, because those who mind don't matter and those who matter don't mind." - Dr. Seuss

I'd been feeling closer to TJ than I had in a long time, and I realized that I loved the companionship and friendship we shared. I couldn't imagine my life without him, and I didn't want to give up on our marriage.

Since apparently I couldn't control my thoughts or feelings about other men, I decided I would control my actions. I would examine and evaluate my thoughts. This would be living with integrity.

In this part of my life, I felt powerless, however. I needed to talk to someone about this. I needed an outside perspective.

It wasn't wrong to have these thoughts, I felt; but why was I attracted to other men? Was this normal? I wondered.

I didn't want to be a cheater. I didn't want to be unfaithful. TJ deserved better.

I spent almost the entire month of June playing victim. I blamed Todd. He had let me down. He hadn't made time to connect with me—and he had left me without a coach. It was his fault.

I enrolled others in my story and they bought in. I felt justified. Without Todd to coach me, I didn't give any more speeches, either.

I sank lower and lower. I got so lost in my story that I didn't realize I was creating my own situation. I knew only that I was unhappy.

Finally, I went to Landmark Education, seeking direction. I'd had enough of wallowing. Since I needed serious help, I signed up for the Advanced Course. Those three days were life changing. As Todd would say, I got "bitch slapped."

We were talking about a point in our lives when we realized we had failed. We would say something to ourselves and that would become our act. To discover what our act was, we did an exercise. On a piece of paper, we wrote, "I am suffering over..." The point was to choose something over which we felt we had lost power. Then we teamed up with a partner and read aloud what we had written. Here's my sob story: I had never felt good enough. I had always needed other people's approval.

I remembered that when I was little, my brothers would run ahead of me when we went hiking on the mountain, and I always felt too slow. I'd get bad headaches and throw up, and my dad would tell me I wasn't in good shape. So, I wasn't good enough to hike, good enough for my dad, good enough for my entire family.

Later, in soccer, I also hadn't been good enough. If I didn't score the most goals in a game, or wasn't the best on the team, I wasn't good enough—and my family never came to any of my games, that I could remember. I wasn't important enough to them.

During this written exercise, I also remembered a few times in school when I didn't understand what we were supposed to be learning. What was wrong with me? I was a dummy. I *had* to be good in school! I *couldn't* fail! School was the only way I bonded with my dad. That's how I knew he loved me.

Then there was the ski team when I was in fourth grade. I was always the last one down the hill. I was scared to ski fast. The entire team would wait at the bottom of the hill for me. How humiliating! Then when I finally made it down, they actually cheered. I was mortified!

On and on the memories came. My whole life, in everything, I had always felt like a failure. My brother Lee became the president of a large company and I was an office manager. I was living below my potential. I never measured up. It was so humiliating. What was wrong with me! I should be successful. I should work harder.

Now here I was trying to become a life coach. Me. Who was I kidding? Myself. I wasn't good at anything. I was never athletic enough. I wasn't cute enough. I wasn't popular enough. I wasn't smart enough. I didn't have friends. I simply wasn't good at anything. My list was pretty morose.

Then, somehow, I had a breakthrough during this furious writing as the memories poured out of me. I felt a shift, something new. For the first time, I could see how I'd made this all up. For some reason, this had become my story. My insight shifted.

"Of course I was good enough for my family," I wrote in the exercise. "I was the special daughter. I was the sister. I was loved. I *am* loved. I *am* good enough. There is nothing wrong with me. My mother loves me. She loves spending time with me. She adores me as I am. She is proud of me. She doesn't think I'm not good enough.

"My little brother Lee loves me. He adores me and loves me. He is proud of me and my life. I'm more than enough. My big brother Ben loved me. I was always his special little sister, and he was so protective of me. He would do anything for me. He always thought I was good enough.

"I *am* good enough for my family. They love me for who I am and who I am not. I have nothing to prove. There is nothing wrong with me. I am enough for me. I am enough for myself. I love myself."

I was amazed at my transformation. The thoughts came so fast that I could hardly keep up with writing them down. By the time I wrote the last line, I felt free.

Then it was time to share.

During sharing with my team partner about all my failures, I discovered that I had told myself whenever I failed at something that I didn't care, that it didn't matter.

That was my act. That was the story I had woven about my life.

Also, whenever I had gotten 90 percent of the way to completing something, I had told myself I didn't want it anymore. This had protected me from possible failure. How silly! I could see it now.

I reveled in this revelation and raised my hand. I was proud of myself. I had discovered my act.

However, when I announced that my act was that I didn't care, the leader looked at me for long moments, then said, "No, I don't think that's it. I think you've been telling yourself that others don't care about you."

That didn't make sense to me, and I shook my head.

She said, "You're not being very coachable."

My heart stopped. I stood there, feeling like an idiot. This was my worst fear. I had no idea what to say. My face turned red. How was I not being coachable? I listened. I was open and honest.

"What are you thinking about me right now?" she asked.

I was clearly thinking, *You don't care about me.* Tears came to my eyes and I cried. I got it. I was afraid that others didn't care.

She smiled and I sat down in awe. I thought about the relationships throughout my life, and I saw the pattern. I had felt that none of them cared about me.

This was a huge realization. I was psyched. I could hardly wait to tell Todd. Then I remembered ... I had walked away from him.

Wait a second, I told myself. *That was part of my act.*

I smiled. I could change this. I had told myself that Todd didn't care about me. Now I knew it wasn't true. I needed to call him, to clear this up.

I waited a few days, to work up the courage. Sitting in my office at work just after lunch, I stared at my cell phone. After what felt like an eternity, I pressed the button.

I got voicemail, so I left a message. Todd called back right away.

When I saw his name flash on my iPhone, my heart raced. My palms sweated.

I picked up the phone, and rambled. "Working with you, Todd, created powerful results for me. I let go of being small. It was amazing. However, I got scared, scared of speaking, scared of really going for it. I tried to make you wrong, like it was your fault. I'm so sorry. I'd put so many expectations on what I thought working with you should be like. When it didn't go that way, I blamed you. I see now that I didn't put a lot of effort into connecting with you. I see that *I* created all the drama. I've been playing victim. I want you to know I'm not going to do that anymore. I want to be real with you. I apologize, Todd. I'm sorry for walking away. I really do care about you." I took a long breath.

Only then did I share my new discovery about my story, which I had learned at Landmark.

Amazingly, Todd wasn't angry with me. He accepted that this was my journey. I wanted to hug him! I laughed with relief. "How do you do that? I want to get to that place. I want to not take things personally and not blame myself for other people's actions."

Todd truly welcomed me back into his life, with an open heart, no grudge, and only loving peace.

"I knew you would call," he said. "We have too much of a connection never to talk again."

Yes, I felt that way, too. And, this time, I would get over myself. I would do whatever it took.

CHAPTER 10
What Lies Within

"What lies behind us and what lies before us are tiny matters compared to what lies within us." - Henry S. Haskins, *Meditations in Wall Street*, 1940

It felt good to be honest with Todd and have him back in my life. Walking away from him had only made me unhappy.

I admired Todd for creating a life he loved. He was being authentic with the people in his life. I committed to creating this in my own life.

For starters, I began to feel a new freedom with Colin. I no longer agonized over what he thought about me. In fact, I no longer felt attracted to him. I had gone from a desperate place and obsession to friendship. Trying to win his approval had been an endless, unrewarding task that had always left me feeling empty.

Now, for the first time, I was able to really open up with him and be my authentic self—the good, the bad, and the ugly.

An amazing thing happened. I began to understand Colin in a way I never had before, and a shift occurred in me. Instead of focusing on how much he cared about *me*, now I concentrated on what I could give back. Crazily enough, that is exactly what I got in return.

Just as Todd was creating a life he loved, I could see that I was starting to do the same for myself. Day by day, I was slowly healing and finding myself happier.

Todd was willing to be my coach again, but I knew I was still too needy for that to work. I was scared of going back down that obsession road. So, I decided having him as a friend was safer.

After completing Landmark's Advanced Course, I was on fire with enthusiasm, inspired and ready to take on the world! I had come a long way, and I knew I could do so much more.

I started with another Landmark seminar, "Excellence in the Zone." It was a three-month commitment and a big deal. The drive time tacked on an additional eight hours to my eight-hour work day. But I was up for it! I wanted big things for my life!

The first night, I sat in the front row. I was all in.

While I waited for the leader to come in and start, a bubbly ball of fire named Alice sat next to me. There was something about her. I commented on her tiger-print purse, and our conversation took off from there. I was so engrossed in talking to Alice that I hardly realized the seminar had started.

The rest of the evening, anytime in the class when we were asked to turn to our partner, Alice and I shared with each other. It was wonderful! I loved this girl! I felt like I'd known her my whole life. I felt so connected and comfortable with her.

At one point, the leader asked for volunteers. She was looking for communicators who would recreate these sessions for people who had been unable to attend. That sounded like a lot of work, a huge commitment on top of my already huge commitment. I had no intention of doing that.

Then Alice leaned over and whispered, "Raise your hand." Without question, I did.

The leader thanked me for volunteering and wrote my name down as a communicator.

What did I just do? Why did Alice ask me to raise my hand? More importantly, why did I? Shit! However, I knew this was all happening for a reason, so I stopped fighting it.

Before the evening was over, the leader asked what each of us was going to create throughout this course. I raised my hand. *Again?* Had I lost control? My hand seemed to fly up on its own, definitely most eager. I even went to the front of the room and told the group I would be motivational speaking. I said that I'd given my first talk a month ago and I wanted to do more. *What had gotten into me?* I wondered. It was as if something inside me was driving me.

The leader asked what I would commit to over the next three months. I was afraid to say too much, so I committed to one more talk.

She said, "I think that's playing small."

I fumed defensively. Did she have any idea how much courage it took for me to get up here and bare my soul? *I don't think so.*

Then I said, "I'm not exactly sure what I want to create as a speaker. I don't want to commit to ten talks, because that would force me down a single road and I'm not sure what I want. I only know that I want to continue speaking ... but I'm unsure of the direction. I just don't want to lock myself in."

She pushed me. "I understand that you don't want to lock yourself into any one thing, but maybe that is exactly what you need to do. Maybe you need to pick a direction and stick with it. It will be hard to get anywhere if, one, you don't start walking and, two, if you walk in circles."

This made sense and I secretly liked that she was prodding me. I had been stuck about how to go forward as a motivational speaker.

"So, you're ready to commit to giving ten talks?" she said.

"Ten? That's way too many. I'm not ready to commit to that." I just looked at her. All eyes were on me. Then, before I knew what was happening, my mouth opened. "Yes, I will commit to giving ten talks by the end of this seminar."

The group clapped and cheered. I swallowed. *Shit. What did I just do?* Nevertheless, it felt good. Hmmm.

Most of the other communicators had completed several other Landmark courses, or had been a communicator before. I didn't have those qualifications. As the leader looked at me, I thought she, too, was wondering why I had volunteered.

Then I realized that communicators were much like coaches. If she had asked for coaches, I certainly would not have raised my hand. However, disguised as "communicating," I was all in. Hmmm. *Curious*, I noted to myself.

I decided that I didn't need a communicator certificate or any more classes. I would recreate the sessions I had already taken, and coach individuals who had missed these classes.

Something else interesting that I discovered about myself: I was good at this. In the majority of my communicator calls, those people had major breakthroughs. They would cry, laugh, or have an incredible "ah-ha" moment. The next week, they would bring up our conversation to the class and share how their lives had moved forward. This didn't just happen once or twice. It happened a lot.

I was coaching! And I was good at it! More importantly, I loved it! An hour felt like minutes. I was so alive!

It's amazing how things can come together. I had enrolled in the seminar and sat next to Alice. She had whispered in my ear ... and I had listened. Now, I was coaching. It was like fate or destiny. I had put out into the universe what I wanted to create ... and the universe had responded. I was in awe.

Several weeks into the course, Alice and I started talking about health and fitness. We discussed excellence, weight loss, and failed diets. I definitely could see that I had created a story around *excellence*—needing to be perfect, to do everything perfectly.

However, in the world of fitness, nothing I had ever done was good enough. I had run a 5K, and it wasn't a long enough race. I had run a 10K, and I wasn't fast enough. I had trained hard and decreased my time; now I wanted to run even faster and do more. Maybe if I did a triathlon?

I had trained all that summer and finished my first triathlon strong—but many other racers had beaten me. I needed to be a little faster.

The next year I was faster, but not fast enough. The third year, I hired a personal trainer; still didn't get there.

I shared this process with Alice. She thought it was ridiculous that I felt inept. "I would love to be able to run a 10K or a triathlon," she said, going on and on about my amazing accomplishments.

To me, it was no big deal. My dad was training to run forty miles. *That* was a big deal.

Then I started to see my absurdity. I could see that my dad didn't think running forty miles was a big deal; because, to him, it wasn't enough. I was chasing excellence ... and I would never get there. I was focused on the outcome, rather than the experience. I wasn't enjoying the *process*. I was accomplishing a lot, but missing the pleasure of it.

I shifted to seeing my fitness as an experience I enjoyed. I could run just because I loved it. It didn't have to be about the clock, or beating someone else. I could run just because of the way it made my body feel: strong, healthy, vibrant. In that instant, running became something I *wanted* to do, for its own sake.

A few weeks later, Alice mentioned that she wanted to run a half marathon. I thought that was very ambitious of her. My dad had run many half and full marathons, and I'd always thought even a half marathon was too far for me. I was a 10K runner, period.

However, as Alice continued to talk about the half marathon, something clicked in me. Alice couldn't currently run the thirteen miles; but she was talking about training, starting small, working her way up to the thirteen miles. That sounded like fun to me, too, and I wanted in.

I had never thought I could run that far. I had always thought how excruciating the last five miles would be. It had always been about finishing the race, the end.

Now, I could see the fun of the process: being outside, spending time with my dog, having fun, being present. For the first time, my fitness was not about the finish line.

I excitedly told TJ my realization. He had run several marathons and knew how to map out a training schedule. He bought a three-month laminated calendar for me and hung it on our bedroom wall. We mapped out my training schedule for the next three months, gradually increasing the miles. By late November, I would be up to the thirteen-mile mark. We scheduled long runs on the weekends and shorter runs during the week.

We wrote down all of the scheduled runs in black; whenever I would complete a run, I would write the actual miles in red. This way, I could see what I accomplished each day.

I shared my goal of running a half marathon with my dad. He was very excited for me. He was currently training to run from one rim of the Grand Canyon to the other rim, then turn around and run back: rim to rim to rim. Our running goals created a special new bond between us. We talked about our running schedules, different runs we had planned, our excitement, and our fears. I had never really understood my dad's passion for long-distance running. It had always seemed so painful. Now, I got it. I had the passion, too.

As I increased the distance of my runs, my confidence also increased. Something inside me was shifting.

The more I ran and the farther I went, the more I enjoyed it. I looked forward more and more to each run. Running was no longer something I had to do. It was something I got to do.

What was happening to me? I had always run only to stay in shape. Now, it was because a peace came over me, a clarity. I came to crave it.

When I was out there, I felt so close to nature. The beauty of the stream, the leaves on the trees, the smell of the grass—it all inspired me! This high was addictive.

I joined my dad on runs. We carried backpacks with water and easily digestible food, mainly baby food. We ran in Moab, Utah—in August. Hot! The water was absolutely essential.

Our first run had a very steep start. The route ascended up the side of a rocky mesa. The face was long and steep. I started to question myself.

As we got closer to the trailhead, my stomach started doing funky flip-flops and panic set in.

"Sure looks steep, doesn't it?" Dad said.

"Shit," I mumbled, and we both laughed.

I would give it my best. I took one step at a time and worked my way to the top. It was tough. My lungs were on fire. Every cell in my body screamed for me to stop. I took it slowly. I drank some water as I went, and focused on what was immediately in front of me.

I focused on the top and gauged my distance from the summit—until I realized I was focusing on the outcome. So I refocused on the process and concentrated on the trail, where I was *now* rather than where I was going. Two things happened. The climb seemed shorter and went quickly, and it was easier and more enjoyable than I had expected. I had feared this hill and doubted my ability to climb it. By taking one step at a time, I found myself at the top of the mesa before I knew it.

When I saw the straight *flat* valley ahead, a rush came over me. I did it! After a few minutes, running on flat ground was effortless.

As my dad and I headed through the valley, my thoughts lessened. I took in the beauty of the red rocks, the glow of the sun, the peace of the meadows. I relaxed into the moment. I could stay here forever.

We ran through the valley and I stopped to wait for my dad. I was so enjoying the solitude that I almost forgot he was back there.

He just smiled at me and beamed. "You get it. You get me."

I did get him. This was quite possibly the closest connection I'd ever felt with him.

We continued our run in silence. In this moment, our relationship transcended. I had spent the majority of my life feeling like something was wrong with me. I had felt out of place and alone. In all of my relationships and friendships, I had not felt anyone understood me. Nobody had gotten me, until Todd.

Now I felt that with my dad, for the first time. I saw love in his eyes. I felt it, too.

Motivational speaking also became easier. In both running and speaking, I pushed the limits. I risked more. I felt braver. More alive!

The magic in both was *presence*. In both, I was in the moment, no thoughts of the past or the future. I now realized the happiness I had sought came from within.

CHAPTER 11

Back Down the Rabbit Hole

"When written in Chinese the word 'crisis' is composed of two characters - one represents danger and the other represents op-portunity." - John F. Kennedy, *address, April 12, 1959*

I could not believe where I was—lying awake in Cortina, Italy. I had no idea what time it was, probably two or three a.m.

Today was my birthday and I was thirty-five. When I was young, I had thought about what it would be like to be old. You know, really old, like thirty-five. I thought life would be so much better.

I had wondered what I would look like, and fantasized that I would be so much better-looking. I would have smooth skin, carry myself with confidence, and be beautiful. My short hair, freckles, and tomboy looks would be way behind me. I would have everything I didn't have as a kid. Mainly, I hoped I would look a lot better as an adult so someone would love me. My husband would be perfect. I would have a family. I would want for nothing.

Now, in a hotel in Italy, I stared at the ceiling. I looked over at TJ, who was sleeping soundly. I felt as lonely as ever. Thirty-five and I was back down the rabbit hole.

Growing up with two brothers, we'd each had our role in the family, labels so we'd know where we fit. My older brother Ben was "the troublemaker."

He got busted for everything. Granted, he was not the smoothest rebel. Once, he carved into our kitchen table. How did our parents know it was Ben? Easy. He carved his own name—at his own place at the table. It was always like that. Ben was always testing, pushing, and trying the limits.

The one thing I get about my big brother today was that he was fearless. Ben was a warrior. He was authentic. He never lied, never faked it, never tried to hide anything. Maybe that was why he was always getting busted. He put it all out there. He lived full out. His butt was always on the line ... and that was the way he wanted it. He lived only eighteen years, but he did more living than I had done in twice that.

As I stared up at the ceiling, I thought back to high school. Another student at our school had been in a car accident as a young kid and severely burned; his face was scarred and deformed. Most of the students were afraid of him. I was. But not Ben. They were close friends. Ben went right up to him and started talking, and he instantly had a friend for life. Their bond was amazing.

One day, this kid came up to me and started talking. As shy as I was, at that time, it was hard for me to feed much into the conversation. So, he did the heavy lifting and, within a few minutes, I was at ease. I realized that his life was so much more than his scars. Before that day, I hadn't seen past them. Now, his courage, spirit, and presence were breathtaking. This was my brother's gift to me, one connection he had made out of so many.

As for me, as a student, I was a nerd. That was my role, "nerd," from kindergarten through high school. I wasn't fun. I had decided I was shy. So, I never had many friends and I didn't talk much. I didn't play sports, musical instruments, or join clubs. I didn't want to participate, and I NEVER raised my hand in class. I never wanted attention drawn to me, and I avoided anything that pushed me in that direction.

I stayed at my little brother's friend's house when my parents would go out of town. The fact that I wasn't staying at a girlfriend's house speaks volumes. I remember once when my parents were on vacation and I was staying there, I was really hungry and wanted an apple but I was terrified to ask for it. Over and over in my mind, I practiced what I would say to his mom. After a couple of hours, I finally got the courage to ask her.

At home, I was the "peacemaker." At least, I wanted to be. I wanted everything to run smoothly, without conflict. By no means was I perfect; I certainly fought with both my brothers, a lot. However, I did as I was told, I didn't break the rules, and I tried to keep our parents happy. I quickly realized that one way to keep them happy, especially my dad, was to get good grades. So, my life's purpose became to study and get good grades ... and the "nerd" was born.

The day I got my first Trapper Keeper, a large notebook, was more exciting than Christmas. For one of my birthdays, I got a complete set of office supplies, including paper shredder, desk lamp, electric stapler, pens, organizers, the works. I was in heaven. Ben put his arm around me and said he was sorry. I looked at him with confusion. He said he couldn't believe how crappy my birthday presents were and he felt so bad for me. We were on opposite ends of the spectrum.

I wish I could say I outgrew this phase. Not even close. After Ben died, I went even further into my shell. I let fewer people in. I studied even harder.

I had one good friend in high school, and we were in all the same classes. At lunch, we took our graphing calculators, connected them and shared programs. That was how I spent my free time. It was fun.

So, where did my little brother Lee fit in? He was "the popular one." From the time Lee could walk, he was charming everyone. It always seemed like things were easy for him. He joined a soccer team and instantly was the captain and the best player. He had just started and, just like that, he was the best.

We all ski-raced growing up and Lee was always the best. From the time our parents put him on skis, he was unstoppable. His room looked more like a trophy case than a bedroom: ribbons, medals, plaques, and glass awards everywhere. It didn't matter what he did, he was just naturally good at it.

It also never seemed like he was my *little* brother. It was always like he'd always had everything figured out. He hung out with kids older than I was, and he was at the front of the social scene at school. He never tagged behind, like other little kids. He never followed. He was always leading.

In true fashion to his nature, although two years younger than me, Lee left home before I did. At fourteen, he went away to school at a ski academy on the East Coast, and he never came back. He never lived in Colorado again. He traveled the world, racing, skiing, and competing. He never seemed to stop.

Today, it still seems like Lee has everything figured out. He still lives on the East Coast, has been married fifteen years, and has a nine-year-old son who is into every sport imaginable. Lee is president of a ski company and on the board of directors for a ski academy. At thirty-three he is at the top. I can only imagine where he will be at fifty.

These places were where we fit, our roles. Ben the rebel, me the nerd, and Lee the charmer. Only one thing set me apart. Good grades. Academics were my arena. School was my thing.

I always told myself it would all work out in the end. When I was at home alone, while they were out with friends, I thought it was okay because I was smart. I was studying, and it would pay off down the road. I clung to that. Someday, I would matter. Someday, I would be heard.

OPTING IN

How was it turning out? Well, here I was, lying in a bed in Italy and feel-ing just as insignificant as I did when I was a kid.

Why is life so hard for me? I worried. *What is wrong with me? Why am I so unhappy? I suck. Period. Thirty-five and I haven't done shit with my life.*

I reminded myself where I was. Italy, for crying out loud! The trip of a lifetime.

Also, dummy, it's your birthday. The one day of the year it's all about you. Celebrate! Be special!

My pep talk to myself helped. Celebrating would snap me out of my funk. So, I got up and dressed.

When I came out of the shower, it was light out now and TJ greeted me cheerfully with a hug. "Happy Birthday!" he announced with joy as he gave me a cute card. It was in Italian so I couldn't read it, but it had a nice picture. I smiled, and I did start to feel genuinely cheerful.

TJ and I ate a quick breakfast at the hotel. Then we planned to walk around town. Cortina was full of ski shops. I actually got fired up.

Then we stepped out into pouring rain, under seriously dreary clouds. We went back inside and got our raincoats, still intent on walking around town. Then we discovered that nothing was open. The town shut down on Sundays. So we looked at store windows for an hour, then went back to our hotel.

That was my birthday. Bummerland.

So, I ate my way across Italy, and my clothes became tighter.

In addition, we stopped at the headquarters where my brother Lee was working. He was in Italy on business and we spent a few days with him.

While I did enjoy Lee's company, I could not stop the comparison game. As he gave us a tour of the facility, it just reminded me how much better he was.

After TJ and I returned home, I decided I needed a new plan. I had been down the rabbit hole before, I told myself. I could pull myself up again.

I decided to continue with Landmark. That would snap me out of my victim mode. I would resume exercise and running, as well as healthier eating. I would *not* give in to depression. I would face it.

No more playing victim! It was time to own my life!

CHAPTER 12
Laughing at My Absurdity

"You may not realize it when it happens, but a kick in the teeth may be the best thing in the world for you." - Walt Disney

Autumn, of all the seasons my favorite.

I sat in Starbucks this October, drinking an Awake tea, and thought about the word *fall*. From the English dictionary: "Move downward ... drop or be lowered ... come down suddenly from upright position ... become less ... be taken by force ... drop to ground in battle ... collapse politically ... display disappointment ... grow sad ... stop to look ... be averted ... sin."

Wow, so many definitions for one word. We think of *fall* and automatically think of negative connotations—as if to fall is a bad thing.

We avoid falling at all costs. From the very start, when we are learning to walk, our main goal is not to fall.

What happens when we fall? A quick and sudden stop of forward motion. Yet we brush ourselves off, get up, and continue going. Sometimes in the same direction; other times not, but we are stronger and wiser. The *fall* has given us something. We are not the same as we were before.

Sipping my tea, sitting in a comfortable chair in the corner, I thought of the great falls in my life: quitting physician-assistant school, landing in the hospital after a night of drinking during college, losing my spot on the college rugby team, considering ending my life ... the list goes on.

Would I change any of those falls? No. They made me the person I am today. Each time, a changed person emerged.

The raw hard truth, the messy and ugly part of life, gives us the best part of who we are: humility, vulnerability, courage, strength, and the knowledge that we can fall *and* emerge. I love the fall!

In the season of fall, hot blazing days to cold nights, the days get cooler and many things start to die. There is a beauty in this transformation.

After two weeks of indulgence in Italy, the season of fall was just in time. I had completed eight of ten talks with my own new company, "Peaks of Excellence." It was scary, but I had done it! I was more capable than I thought.

Now I could feel it was time for a leap, a jump, maybe a fall.

I enrolled in the communication course at Landmark, "Access to Power," which started the first week of October. I also hired Todd to work with me again. It was time to face my fear of losing him, of his leaving me.

Through this new Landmark course, I came to realize that I had forced the outcome in my relationship with Todd and others. When things had gotten tough or not gone my way, I had withdrawn. I had done this with TJ, with Colin, and my dad, among many.

With Colin, I had desperately wanted to be close. Whenever I didn't feel it was going that way, I had distanced myself emotionally. When I had taken a risk to be closer to him and didn't feel him matching my interest, I had retreated. I had played that cycle hundreds of times over the eight years of working with him.

I had also done this with TJ, thousands of times, almost daily. I always had an idea of how I wanted things to go. When they didn't, I blamed TJ and wouldn't even speak to him. No matter how big or small the infraction, I withheld my affection. Once I began to see this pattern with TJ, I laughed at myself. I was behaving absurdly. I had thought everything wrong in our marriage was TJ's fault. When he wouldn't park where I thought he should, I just expected him to know. When he would drive past the spot, my anger would build. Then when he *finally* parked, I would be furious and not talk to him during the entire outing. Poor TJ!

Now, I could see this pattern in most of my relationships. I would get all upset. But now I knew they were not to blame. It was me, all me. Realizing that, now I also knew I could change it. I would!

So, I analyzed myself. Why did I withdraw? Why did I push people away? I really wanted to be a friend. I really wanted to open up. So, I would, now. I would no longer be afraid.

I would start by strengthening my genuine new friendship with Colin, because I still tended to shut down with him at times. So I called and we talked for a long time.

Just as we were hanging up, he said, "Wait, I'd really like to have more time to talk."

Okay. So we set up a dinner.

It was that easy? I had struggled to be Colin's friend for years. Now, when I stopped forcing, it was suddenly effortless ... and all I had done was listen. Wow. Listen? Maybe I had never really listened to him.

I began to realize a new way of communicating: listening, caring about what others have to say. I made amazing strides with Colin, and I wanted to continue this trend with others. Next was Todd.

115

I had my first coaching call coming up again with Todd and I began to feel nervous about it. I decided to clear my head by taking Lucy for a walk. I grabbed her leash and headed out.

It was a beautiful crisp fall afternoon. We headed up our usual route and I took in the beauty of the autumn colors among the Colorado aspens. I thought about what I wanted to create now with Todd as my coach again. Was it something to do with motivational speaking?

No, I answered myself.

I stopped. "No?"

How could it not be public speaking? Perplexed, I stared off into space. Lucy nudged me, and we continued our walk. She bounded up the trail.

I'm no longer interested in motivational speaking? I thought, dumbfounded. What did that mean ... and why not?

It just doesn't seem fun right now, I answered myself.

"Not fun?" Now, this I really had to process. What was going on here with me? Why had I wanted to do motivational speaking in the first place?

As early as kindergarten, I had been in awe of public speakers. I had always admired and respected the people at the front of the room. So, that was the job I had wanted.

Then it came to me. All my life I had been looking for respect ... and that would lead to love... ah-ha!

Lucy and I headed up the trail toward the wide, open meadow. Why was I searching so desperately for love? I wondered, as we walked through the beauty. *Because I never really felt I was loved*, I answered myself.

I thought back to my childhood. Believing myself to be shy, I had taken myself out of all life's games. I hadn't participated in anything. Then when Ben died, I became "the terrible person." And the rape during college meant I was weak, clearly unlovable.

I had withdrawn to avoid the pain, to escape the rejection. I had been living in the dark. Ever since, I had not let anyone in.

Now, suddenly, the lights were on. In this bright light, I got that my dad had loved me all along. I had been searching for his love. I already had it.

This was intense, almost too much. Tears rolled down my cheeks. In the meadow with Lucy, I thought of the magnitude of TJ's love for me.

Lucy looked up at me quizzically and I laughed. We both picked up our pace, and my thoughts and feelings tumbled.

I had been fighting the marriage. I had been resisting everyone who had ever tried to love me. A huge smile swept across my face. Now I would love my life!

CHAPTER 13
The Land of Should

"It is our choices ... that show what we truly are, far more than our abilities." - J. K. Rowling

As part of the "Access to Power" Landmark course, I had one of their coaches helping me, too. I figured I needed all the help I could get. We set up a couple of short coaching calls.

I shared with her my breakthrough about love. She was moved. "So, what are you going to create?" she asked.

My excitement drained right out of me. I didn't know.

"Well, what are you up to?" she prompted.

I'd been motivational speaking, but now I wasn't sure whether to continue with it.

"You can pick a new direction," she said.

"I'm not sure what that is."

"Well, just pick something, anything. What's the first thing that pops into your mind?"

I hesitated. I wasn't comfortable saying anything. "I don't want to be stuck with something I'm not committed to. I want to be careful with my word."

"No problem. You won't be stuck with it. Just tell me what's coming to your mind, anything."

I wanted to shout, *I don't know!* Why was she making me feel wrong? Why did I have to create anything in this moment?

Finally, I gave in. "Well, if I have to pick something, I would say working with kids."

I shocked myself. I had no clue where that came from. That hadn't been on my radar. Hmmm.

"Wow. That's excellent," she said. "I really hear commitment and excitement in your voice."

Was she kidding? Commitment in my voice? I didn't know if I wanted to do this at all. I was just trying to make her happy.

"Tell me more about working with kids," she said. "What would that look like?"

"I don't know. Maybe creating fun and celebrations, helping kids create joy and love in their lives." I was making this up as I went.

"Excellent!" she answered. "I really feel you have a passion for this. You could really make a difference. You're amazing."

So much for throwing out ideas. I was *not* inspired. I had *no* clue! I still felt trapped.

I sat there, confused, and harangued myself. Why did I feel so bad? I felt a weight on my chest, so much pressure that I could hardly move, frozen, as if my life had just been sucked out of me.

I had just realized I *am* loved and already I was beaten down? Maybe this was one fall from which I would never get up.

The next morning, I barely mustered the energy to get out of bed. I went downstairs and made myself a cup of Awake tea. As I stood there waiting for the water to boil, I looked over at the couch. Every part of my being wanted to crawl up into a little ball on that couch and not move.

I called Colin and asked for the day off, feigning exhaustion. It didn't feel good to lie.

He laughed. "Sure, get some rest. I'll catch up with you tomorrow."

I spent the rest of the day on that couch, through two seasons of *Nip/Tuck* on mindless TV.

My little voice also kept me company all day. *What a waste of time. You're being lazy. You are not creating anything.* Admittedly, this was not my wise voice -- it was the harpy one.

I kept thinking about why I was in the world. What *did* I want to create? It seemed too much. I couldn't even summon up the energy to get off the couch. How could I make a difference in the world?

I lay there, feeling worse and worse. The longer I stayed, the harder it was to move.

At one point in the afternoon, I did manage to walk to my computer to write. That was the LEAST I could do. I forced myself to open my laptop, and I dreaded the blank page.

The machine roared to life. It wasn't until then that I remembered my book was on a thumb drive, in my wallet. *Okay, where the hell is my wallet?*

I went to my dresser, where I usually left it. It wasn't there. I looked in the car ... nope. I checked my clothes from the day before; nothing.

Anger started to rage. "Why the fuck is everything so difficult!"

I stormed back to my office and kicked the door, hard. Ouch! The door banged against the wall. For a brief second, I did feel better.

But then I sank even lower. I couldn't remember the last time I had done anything in anger, let alone kicked something. What was going on with me?

I headed back to the couch and spent the rest of the day right there. Happiness would never be a permanent fixture in my life, I realized. I was sentenced to despair. It was the only world I knew. It clutched at me— like I was its prey.

The next morning, I had a scheduled call with Todd, and here I was, right back where I'd started: depressed, deflated, pathetic. My whole body tensed as I called him. My stomach turned with nausea.

"Good morning," Todd said loud and clear.

Right in that moment, I felt better. His voice was a source of comfort. He didn't judge me. I was going to be okay. I took a deep breath. "Good morning."

"How are you?" he asked.

God, where to begin? "I'm better," I choked out.

"Better?"

"Yeah." I could feel the tears coming. "I don't feel good, actually."

"Mentally or physically?"

I tried to hold back my tears. "About my life." The tears came anyway.

"Got it. What is it you're not feeling good about?"

"I'm supposed to know what I want to do—but I don't know. I have no idea. I do want to contribute to the world, but how?"

"Got it. What's changed? The other day, this wasn't showing up for you at all."

I filled him in. He asked if the Landmark coach was helping me. I instantly shot back, "No, I feel so much worse."

"Then get rid of her," he said matter-of-factly. Like, duh, of course.

Funny, so simple. I hadn't thought of that as an option. Instantly, I felt better.

Todd reminded me of my incredible journey. I thought back to all my breakdowns, breakthroughs, and transformations, and the dark place where it had all started. Now I could see how far I had come.

"Molly, you can take a rest. You can take time to have fun."

A smile swept across me. I could... There was no rush. The weight lifted from me. I could breathe! I laughed joyously.

"It's good to hear you laugh."

I basked in my refound joy. "It feels good."

Somewhere along the way, I had gotten lost in the land of "should." It had crippled my enthusiasm and inspiration.

Now, again, I was free to all possibilities.

CHAPTER 14
High on Possibilities

"Thou shalt not be a victim. Thou shalt not be a perpetrator.
Above all, thou shalt not be a bystander."
- Holocaust Museum, Washington, DC

The *shoulds* were gone, but I didn't know what to do with the rest of my life.

I had invited several people to the completion of my Landmark communication course, so I felt I *must* go. The shoulds were back.

My mom, TJ, and I arrived a few minutes early. He had attended several completion nights, so he was familiar with the routine. I was very excited to show my mom my new journey. I had grown so much. I had spent many hours here over the last six months.

We ran into several people I knew. I gave them hugs and we caught up. I was in love with the energy of the room! Mom commented on the light in my eyes and my sparkle.

But halfway through the evening, I was ready to bail. On an incredibly long break at 8:30 p.m., I realized that if we left now, I could be in bed by eleven. The idea of bed sounded really good.

I turned to my mom and realized she was very engaged in a story she was telling *me*. I had been tuning her out. She was actually enjoying the evening ... and I was off in my future plans.

So many times in my life I had gone 90 percent of the way, then stopped. Now was the time to change that pattern.

I changed my attitude and got back into the evening's activities. I shared with the group what had shown up for me regarding love in my life, like realizing that my dad does love me. I felt everyone's love toward me from the room.

As I walked back to my seat, the back row stood and all raised their hands to the ceiling, raising the roof for me. Wow. The evening got better from there.

Next, we had an exercise on acknowledgment. I turned to a complete stranger and acknowledged her. I really listened to her, and a connection formed, in seconds. *If I did this with everyone,* I thought, *what would the rest of my life be like?*

TJ, my mom, and I drove home hours later. It was like no time had passed at all. We were full of possibility.

I was excited about my next coaching call with Todd. I had been writing all week and was well on my way with my running. I was creating my new world! No more sad stories!

The conversation with Todd migrated to my job. I didn't like my job, and I wasn't prepared for that discussion. I was bored with the job. Very bored. The employees were all so negative, and I felt stuck. I showed up every day, uninspired, even though I was in a good place with Colin.

"What can you do about that?" asked Todd.

I was resigned not to think about the job. I had no intention of changing it—or discussing it with Todd. He was supposed to be helping me with my life and my book.

"Isn't your job a part of your life?" he asked.

Well, yeah. So, I shared how I felt trapped.

"Do you get that you are responsible?" he pointed out.

It was like he'd just punched me in the stomach. *What the fuck?* All the work I'd done to own my life and I was still a victim? Shit, shit, shit. This was like a cancer. Just when I'd thought I was in remission, SLAM, the cancer had spread.

I fumed, not so much at Todd as at myself for not noticing. I was even more angry because I knew *why* I was stuck in the job. Fear of saying no to Colin. Fear of really going for my dream. Why couldn't I be fearless? Why wasn't I?

I felt sick. Yet remaining a victim was *not* an option.

I hung up, knowing I was going to take the leap, although terror engulfed me. What would come next?

I had an eight-mile run scheduled for today. I certainly didn't feel like hammering out my writing, so I ran.

I didn't bundle up, only running clothes, and the crisp air hit me. It was cold as shit outside! I wanted to go back to bed. However, Lucy looked up at me with her big brown eyes, so my feet hit the pavement firmly.

Within minutes, the sun came out and the beauty of autumn embraced me ... and there was nowhere else I wanted to be.

The more I ran, the better I felt; Lucy, beside me, was just as eager. Todd had asked me about the runner's high. It's the point where you no longer realize you're running. The miles peel away and there's nowhere else you want to be. The rush of the energy courses through all your cells, every nerve.

Suddenly, you can do anything! You're a little kid with steps quickened, thanking God that you are alive!

I walked another mile to cool down. I wasn't ready to go back inside. My thoughts drifted to the conversation with Todd, and I made a choice. I would stay at the job, but I would make it better. If there was a problem at work, I was the problem. If I was bored, it was up to me to create fun and excitement. It was a challenge, but I was up to it.

I would sit with each staff member and create a project with him or her. I would enroll each person in how, together, we could better serve the patients. I would empower them to come up with their own ideas, and I would support their ideas. At the end of the year, we would re-evaluate. We had all gotten complacent. It was time to shake things up.

I looked forward to Monday morning! I was excited!

It was one of the best Mondays of my life. It felt like a completely different job. The phones rang like crazy, patients were piled up in the waiting room, all the staff needed my attention, at once. I loved it!

We had been struggling to make payroll. Today, there was not one empty spot in the schedule, and five surgery cases were scheduled for tomorrow. On top of that, patients couldn't seem to pay their bills fast enough and we took in double our normal revenue.

With a shift of my attitude, everything had changed. I had *chosen* to no longer be a victim. I had refused to feel helpless. I had created something different!

128

OPTING IN

The staff was on fire. The energy was electric. And this was only Monday.

Amidst this swarm of activity, I found myself in grace, handling every-thing with ease. It was like a dance. I just sailed through it, in rhythm, in harmony, in the zone.

Tuesday was even better. My father-in-law decided he was done with ly-ing in bed and wanted to go to dinner. That doesn't sound like much, but he was eighty-six and had open-heart surgery a month ago, a valve replaced and arteries cleaned out. Since the surgery, he had refused to eat, drink, or get out of bed. He also had been back to the hospital several times for fluids and had lost a substantial amount of weight. TJ was scared.

Then Monday night, it was like the flip of a switch. One day, TJ's dad was uninspired. The next, he got up, dressed, and announced that he wanted to go out!

I did propose project ideas to the staff, individually, and I listened to them. I was floored! It was as if we had been speaking two different languages and had finally gotten a translator. Clearly, their concerns had weighed on their minds. I now gave them a say in how to best perform their jobs.

As I explained my ideas to them, one at a time, their faces lit up, their lights turned on. Amazing ideas poured from them. I was dumbfounded by how effortless this was. All I had to do was listen. Their enthusiasm had been there all along. All I had to do was invite their participation, involve them. It was like they had been waiting for me to say *Go*. Once I did, they were unstoppable.

No more idle moments for any of us. We had so much we wanted to do. It reminded me of the Rolling Stones song, "If you start me up, if you start me up, I'll never stop." I was on a roll.

CHAPTER 15
Seeing with New Eyes

"Every adversity, every failure, every heartache carries with it the seed on an equal or greater benefit." - Napoleon Hill

I opened my eyes and looked around. It was dark and quiet outside, but something had wakened me. Not the rain.

I looked over at the nightstand. My iPhone was lit. Someone had called or texted.

In that instant, the peace of my sleep was gone and I remembered what I had done. TJ was gone.

It was a text from Colin. He was in the hospital, just out of surgery, yet *he* wanted to help *me*.

I had been at the hospital all day with him for his shoulder surgery, an old injury that had never healed correctly. The surgery had gone fine, no complications. I was sitting in Colin's hospital room, when he looked over and asked, "Are you okay?"

I had been crying. I didn't want to overwhelm him with my own pain. However, the words were out before I knew it. "TJ and I are taking a break." Colin's eyes got big and I saw concern on his face.

"Mol, I'm sorry."

"It's been a tough day ... but I'm okay," I mumbled. I wasn't sure I *was* okay.

"So, what happened?" he asked groggily.

I took a deep breath and recounted the events of the morning. I hadn't slept well; rain pounding on the roof had kept waking me. Worried about Colin's surgery, I had gotten up at 5:30 and made tea. Then I'd sat at the computer and started writing. At first, the words came slowly, but then I'd started to enjoy myself.

I was typing away when TJ came in and said good morning. We'd already said good morning, so I was annoyed to be disrupted in the middle of my writing. Didn't he understand this was MY time?

My progress was shot, my happiness vanished. I didn't say anything back to TJ, and he walked out of the office unaware of how I was feeling.

I finished my hour of writing, then put on my running clothes. Lucy knew my routine and jumped up and down with anticipation. Seeing her so full of energy brought a smile to my face. She got so excited every single time.

I was heading out the door when TJ came down in his biking clothes. "Hold up, I'll come with you."

I took a deep breath and waited for him, my irritation building. I had only one hour to be outside and enjoy the day, and the minutes were ticking by.

Outside, the cold blast was piercing. "Shit, it's cold out here." My muscles were tight, and my first steps were slow and labored.

As my body began to warm, my pace picked up and I looked forward to losing myself in the run. However, just then, TJ started asking questions. I slowed and looked back, so he could hear my answers, which ruined my pace and my moment. Also, on this rocky uneven section of the trail, I needed to watch where I was going.

So, the conversation with TJ was awkward. He was back there on his bike, and he kept trying not to hit the back of my feet.

"Let's just talk later," I yelled back to him.

"What?" he hollered.

I repeated myself, with frustration.

"Oh, okay," he said, "we'll talk when we get to the pavement."

We arrived at the pavement. So much for the fun part of my run. Lost.

I leashed Lucy and headed up the paved road. Normally, I would run a few miles up, then turn and run back; it was just enough of a slope to keep me slightly winded. However, as TJ and I started up the road, he resumed the conversation, and my irritation grew. It was hard to talk slightly out of breath, and difficult to say too many words at once while trying to maintain a pace. Didn't he get that this was important to me? That this was MY routine and I needed to maintain it?

The more we talked, the more I got out of my zone. I so longed for it, and it was not happening.

My second irritation: TJ's hearing loss. He could barely hear me even in a quiet room, and now he wasn't wearing his pair of $6000 hearing aids, so what good were they? He was ruining my day!

Third, Lucy was now on the leash and it was difficult with the bike right behind her. She kept jerking on the leash when the bike got too close, which pulled on my arm and shoulder.

Fourth, TJ's fucking mountain bike. It was noisy, the chain rattled, the brakes squeaked—and I had asked him several times to get it fixed. I tried to tune it out. It just seemed louder.

At the top of the road, we turned to head home. I was looking forward to the downhill, where I could catch my breath and enjoy running. But, downhill, TJ's bike rolled even faster. Squeak, squeak, squeak. Fucking brakes!

I was holding Lucy's leash. When TJ got too close, she lurched. Squeak, jerk, lurch. Squeak, jerk, lurch. The squeaking brakes were all I could hear! It was like fingernails grating across a chalkboard.

After we were back home, I asked myself: Why was I so mad? Why had I woken up so unhappy? Why was I having highs, then quickly losing the glow? I'd had several breakthroughs, spent days on a high, then would come crashing down. Why?

Instantly, I knew, and it made me feel icky. There was one common denominator: TJ.

I panicked. No, no, no, that couldn't be it!

Shut down.

But I could not avoid the thought. It kept popping into my mind.

Was divorce the brave and fearless thing to do? I fretted. Would that be running away? Again, on the up-and-down roller coaster. Just when I thought I was past it.

I continued my story to Colin in his hospital room, telling him how I had then called Todd and tried to explain how I was feeling about TJ, and relayed the bike story.

"Do you adore TJ?" Todd had asked me.

I thought about it. In my silence, Todd continued. "My wife lights up the room. All the little things she does are so cute and I love that about her. I love her. I adore her."

Every ounce of hope drained out of me then, as I realized that every little thing TJ did annoyed me. I loved him, but I did not adore him. Oh, my.

"Could I come to adore TJ?" I asked Todd. "Can I get the attraction back?"

"Man, if I had the answer to that one, I wouldn't be talking to you right now. I'd be rich," Todd answered.

All hope trickled out of me.

I hung up with Todd without an answer.

Action seemed a better plan than no action, so I decided to tell TJ I needed a break. That would catapult me out of victim status. That would give me control over myself and my life.

Yet sadness engulfed me. I loved TJ, I really did. I cared for him. However, I did not light up when he walked into a room. My heart did not skip a beat whenever TJ called. I lit up *his* world. He did not light up mine. I didn't feel for him the way he felt for me.

After the run this morning, after I had berated TJ in my mind for disrupting my joy and my routine, he had looked at me with adoration and said, "You're so cute. I'm the luckiest man to be married to you."

I just smiled and said, "Thanks."

Now what was I supposed to do with that?

Guilt haunted me. I should feel differently, I told myself. I should act differently with TJ. I should love him more. I should be happy. Should, should, should.

I was not, and I couldn't remain with TJ one more minute. I couldn't stand feeling wrong. I needed time out.

So, I walked downstairs to find TJ, my heart in my stomach, ready to throw up or cry or both. I just wanted it over. I wanted what Todd had with his wife, something other than what I had.

I found TJ reading on the couch. He looked so happy and content. It broke my heart, and I almost changed my mind.

No! I need to be strong. Fearless! I commanded myself.

"We need to talk," I squeaked out to TJ.

"Okay, what's on your mind?"

"I want to take a break." There, it was out.

"What? From me?"

The confusion on TJ's face tore at me. "Yes, a break from our marriage. I'm not happy, and I don't know what else to do." The tears started to come.

"What do you want me to do?" he asked sincerely.

"I need some space, some distance, some time."

Suddenly, TJ was angry. "This makes no sense at all! You're all over the map! One day, you're fine. The next, you want a divorce. I don't think you know what you want!"

He was right. I didn't. Up, down, up, down. I was a mess. I was crazy. This was just my best guess at the time.

After several pleas and many times of repeating that I simply wasn't happy, TJ agreed to give me space. He would spend time at our house in Moab, Utah. He would pack a bag and be gone before I got back from the hospital. I walked out the front door without looking back. I couldn't. At every turn, TJ had thought about me. He had always put me first. He adored me and would do anything for me, including move out.

Why didn't I feel like that! Every time TJ did something nice for me, it only made me feel worse. I hated the way I treated him. I hated who I was when I was with him.

The only thing that brought me comfort as I drove to the hospital was the old adage "sometimes it has to get worse before it gets better." Maybe that was what was going on? Maybe, eventually, I *would* feel better.

I finished telling Colin about my breakup with TJ just as other people came into the room to see him. I was relieved by the interruption. I sat in the room for a while. Then, suddenly, I missed TJ—desperately. I told Colin I needed to go home. He said he would call me tomorrow and he gave me the best hug he could, hooked up to many machines.

I ran out of the hospital. Sitting in the dark parking lot, I cried so hard that I could barely catch my breath. Then, shaking, I drove home slowly.

TJ's car was gone when I arrived. I was hoping he'd ignored what I'd said.

Lucy greeted me with her usual exuberance. When I turned on the light, I saw the note TJ had left on the kitchen counter, saying he was sorry. *He was sorry? I* was the asshole. What the hell was wrong with me!

I went straight to bed, curled up in the blankets, and buried my head in the pillows. I wanted a hug. The bed was so huge and empty. I was so cold that I could not get warm. I curled in a tight ball and cried myself to sleep.

Then I was reading Colin's text and listening to the rain. I felt like I had the flu.

It rained on and off all morning. That's how I felt, too.

I didn't feel like my usual morning run, but maybe it might help. So, when there was a break in the rain, I grabbed Lucy on her leash and we headed out.

I was winded even running downhill. Of course, Lucy decided she needed to poop before we reached her normal spot. I picked up the poop with the baggie from my jacket and carried the bag with me.

A few blocks down the road, we reached the dirt trail that would have a trash can en route. So I carried the bag in my leash hand and we continued running.

The next thing I knew, we were back at the end of the dirt section and I was still carrying the poop bag. I had carried it the entire trail. My shit, so to speak.

At the next mile or so down the trail, when I stopped, I realized that my breathing was labored even though I had run mostly downhill.

Nevertheless, I continued another few miles. At the intersection to the other side of town, again I noticed I was breathing heavily. What the heck? My heart rate was way high and I felt like I was going to throw up. Lucy kept looking up at me with inquisitive eyes. She didn't understand why I was so slow today. Neither did I.

OPTING IN

I waited for the light to change, then ran across the intersection. Then I walked to catch my breath. I felt better, so we ran a bit farther. Then I needed to stop again. Lucy was baffled.

I never found my groove. Something was wrong. I thought back to what I had last eaten. It had been a while, and nothing yesterday. Well, no wonder. No fuel.

I fought the urge to run home. After some arguing with myself, I decided walking would be more enjoyable. After all, the goal was really to have more fun, to be outside. It was about the journey, not the destination or how fast I got there.

So I walked, and Lucy loped alongside me.

This crazy back-and-forth arguing with myself about walking or running was another defining moment in my life: realizing it was okay to walk, that I didn't always *have* to be running. Life was not always a marathon, even though it felt that way.

Walking had always felt like failure to me. Yet, today, it was perfect.

I found myself noticing many things: the beauty of the morning, dew on the leaves, kids playing soccer. I also noticed that I was happy.

Did I want TJ walking with me? No. Was I happy alone? In this moment, yes. Wow. I used to be alone all the time, but I had never liked it. Something about me had changed. In this moment, I actually felt good. This was new. For most of my life I hadn't liked myself. I had felt ugly and that no one liked me.

Was that why I had been desperate to get married? Yes. I didn't want to be alone. If someone married me, that would mean I wasn't ugly and awful. I had gotten married to be happy ... but I wasn't happy.

Well, no wonder I was struggling with the marriage. No wonder TJ was confused. *He* hadn't changed. I had. I had started out needing him, yet I had come to resent him. For our entire marriage of five years, he had tried to reassure me, and it was never enough.

Running had been the metaphor for my life. Early in our marriage, I had been afraid of running. I was afraid of being alone. I had asked TJ to come along. I wanted him close to me. Then when I started running with my dad, running became a thing in itself—the one place where I felt like me.

TJ was trying to fit in, but he didn't fit. Now that I knew how to swim, he was drowning me. I no longer *needed* him.

If I was going to find happiness, it was in myself. I could stop running—running away from life.

I had an epiphany. My happiness depended on *me*, and I could slow down.

CHAPTER 16
Those Lovin' Feelings

"It always seems impossible until it's done." - Nelson Mandela

I am the source of my own happiness. Got it.

What if I could do this in my marriage? What if I could still make it work with TJ? My stomach hurt just thinking about this.

No, I will not do this to myself again! I declared. *I cannot go back. It's impossible.*

To be fair, TJ wouldn't go back either, not to the way things were. The transformation in him these last two weeks was phenomenal. He was a new person. He was himself. He was showing up in the world as TJ. It was good to see. He, too, had lost himself in the marriage. I loved witnessing the new zest and light in his eyes, the new spark.

The first week after TJ left, he had been a wreck. He had thought his life was over, and he didn't know how to be without me. He was in a depressed stupor. I was the bad guy, the enemy. He blamed me for being bipolar, for being in love with someone else, for being emotionally unstable. This was all my problem and I needed to get over it.

We spent the first week with no contact. I had asked TJ not to call me and to give me space. He had honored my request.

The second week, we started to talk. I talked to him on the phone several times and I could sense a shift in him. The anger and blame were gone. He told me he'd been scared of losing me and had been paralyzed with fear. The more he had worried about losing me, the tighter he had held on—until I could no longer breathe. He finally saw that.

He also got that he had lost himself somewhere along the way; that he, too, was not happy in the marriage. He also wanted something different for his life. He also wanted to be happy.

TJ told me he enrolled himself in the Landmark Forum. I couldn't have been more surprised. I had asked him several times about going and he had always resisted. Now he had signed up all on his own. This was shocking. This was new.

His breakthroughs were unbelievable and they just kept coming. He discovered that in our marriage, he had tried to be the good guy, to take care of me, fix me (feel righteous). He, too, had needed to feel loved, and we were both miserable.

He also realized that he had lost interest in many of his passions and his friends. He hadn't done anything that was not initiated by me. He had lived our entire marriage to make *me* happy. He had forgotten about himself.

Now, TJ wanted to reconnect with his buddies. He made plans to fish, hike, bike, ski, pursue photography. He started volunteering. He committed to working with young kids in the outdoors. It was heartening to see him blossom.

I held open a space in my heart for TJ if he ever wanted to call about his new adventures and the people in his life. He did, and it was fun to hear his excitement. I was so happy for him. I wanted only the best for him. I absolutely did.

He flew to Ohio to see his family, reconnected with his brother in Colorado, signed up for a photography class in Moab.

We were still married. So, I didn't know what would happen next. I had no answers. I only had hope ... and I was happy. We were both testing our wings, learning to be ourselves.

We were living separately, for now at least. I kept the house. Lucy stayed with me. TJ moved to our house in Moab. It felt good to be responsible for my own life. I liked my own company.

I enjoyed being in the mountains, and I continued to work with Colin. Things were still going well at the job. The employees were excited about their projects, and the difference in our customer service was astounding. With the employees happy, this translated directly to a better experience for our patients.

I still pondered the question of whether I wanted to be alone. I was happy in my new life, but I was lonely and I missed being held. I missed coming home to someone and holding hands. Did I want this with TJ? I didn't know.

Actually, I was afraid of getting close to TJ again. I didn't want to lose my happiness again. The thought was terrifying.

Was I ready to give up on the marriage? I wondered. I wasn't sure. Was I ready to have TJ back home? No. Did I want to live alone the rest of my life? Also no.

Where did this leave me? Stuck. I didn't want to live without TJ. I didn't want to live with him. What did I want? It was dizzying to contemplate.

I will never know if I will be happy with TJ unless I try, I told myself. Maybe I could create something new with him? I wanted to laugh with him again. To hike, ski, giggle, explore, travel, be spontaneous, have fun! I wanted to take us lightly and not be so serious. I wanted to flirt again. I wanted to fall back in love. I wanted to adore TJ again. I wanted to light up when he walked into the room. Could I have that again? Could I get it back?

I wished we could start over. I missed the flutter in my heart. I dreamed of a new proposal from TJ. This time, with fresh-fallen snow and red roses, riding in a horse-drawn carriage, a blanket over our laps, both of us deliriously in love.

While I was coming to peace with TJ, it was anything but that with Todd. My life felt like the kids' game Chutes and Ladders. I'd get up a couple of rungs, then fall down twice as many. Just when I'd start to feel happy in one part of my life, another would fall apart. Slam, back down again.

Then I had a crystal-clear dream about Todd. When I woke, it was so clear in my mind and the feelings were still very vivid. I felt very connected to him.

I dreamed I was in the military, going from station to station during orientation and boot camp, and I took whatever they dished out. It wasn't good or bad, it just was. At times, I was yelled at, ordered what to do, shuffled place to place. I was okay with it all.

Then I looked around and everyone was shaving their heads. I was excited. I'd always wanted to shave my head and never had the guts to do it. Now I could.

I was making my way up in line, when I looked over and saw Todd. He was shaving his head, but his razor had an attachment to it; as he cut his hair, his hair was much longer than everyone else's and no one seemed to notice.

He looked over at me and I made my way to his line. I was excited to know someone here, especially someone higher in the ranks and in charge. When I made it to the front of the line, we didn't say anything to each other; we didn't have to. I sat and he cut my hair using his special razor. He winked at me, and my hair looked good when it was done. Then he held my arm, and I knew I was safe with him here. He was looking out for me. I felt so close to him. We had a bond.

I didn't tell Todd right away about this dream. I worried that he might know how I felt about him, and I didn't want to lose him as my friend and life coach.

But when we started our weekly call the next Friday, I found myself telling him, excited about the connection we had shared in the dream.

"Uh-oh," he said.

"No, it's not bad!" I shot back, regretting I had said anything at all. I described the dream, about the hair and all, hoping he would get that he had just made me feel safe.

Immediately, I felt his distance.

No!

I accused him of not listening. He apologized and backed up.

The truth is *I* wasn't listening to him. I was withdrawing, my old habit. Back to square one. Back down the rabbit hole. *Shit.*

The next day was the weekend and I went for a long run with Lucy. I felt strong, and the miles cleared my mind. It felt like I could run forever.

It was Halloween, so that evening I went over to visit Colin. I helped him with the physical therapy exercises for his shoulder and I ended up staying the rest of the day. Our conversation was amazing. We talked about life, death, family, love, loss, anxiety, and more. I felt so open with him! We talked for hours and I felt I really got him. We could talk about anything, everything. I felt that he got me, too. That he heard me. I felt heard.

I realized I wasn't *attracted* to him, though. I didn't have thoughts of wanting to sleep with Colin. I was just with him and it was beautiful. It was a perfect day.

Todd didn't get me, but Colin did. I thought that was enough. It wasn't.

By Monday morning, I was fully, completely back down the rabbit hole, my mind in overdrive. My conversation with Todd could have meant a thousand different things. *Why* did he not get me? Did he not care? What had I done wrong? Why had I told him the stupid dream?

I'm such an idiot!

I desperately wanted this madness to end. Why couldn't I let this go and stop thinking about Todd?

Please, please, please, make this stop!

I sent him an e-mail.

> Todd, I feel like something is off, something is different. Our last conversation felt very different from the others. I guess if there was one thing, I would say your *listening* felt different.
>
> I just erased that line about twenty times. I've been staring at this e-mail for forty-five minutes.

I'm scared to tell you what's on my mind. I'm afraid of what you'll think of me. I thought of calling, but it's too late. I thought of deleting this altogether. I guess the best thing is to be brave and just get real with you.

I tried to explain the connection I felt to you in the dream, because I'd felt *gotten* by you. It was an amazing closeness. Then you were so distant on the phone.

Feeling close to you is what allowed me to be so open with you and created a power for me in our work together.

My commitment to this process is to be honest and raw. I'm struggling with the words now, because I feel like something is off. I don't feel you get me.

Does any of this make sense? I don't ever want to be afraid to talk to you, Todd, or tell you what's on my mind.

Molly

It took me over three hours to write that e-mail. I thought it would ease my anxiety. It didn't. I was on the brink. I *was* attracted to Todd.

The next morning, I had an answer.

Hi, Molly, I completely get what you are saying, specifically the dream and its significance. Yes, it took me a while to really hear you. For that, I apologize. We do have a very special connection. I couldn't agree more. It is a very special relationship.

I did feel I was hearing you by the end of the conversation. If not, let's talk about it. Please call me.

Thanks for being honest. That's always where a true connection starts. There will never be a time when you can't say what's so for you—at least with me. You haven't hurt my feelings, or offended me. That's just not the place I come from as a human being.

Love, Todd

I felt better. I realized that I had needed to hear Todd say our relationship was special and that we had a connection. I also realized that now I could tell him how I felt about him. It was time to be brave.

CHAPTER 17
Stopping the Maddening Thoughts

"I never lie because I don't fear anyone.
You only lie when you're afraid." - John Gotti

I was restless this night early in November and I didn't sleep well. I kept waking up. Then it would take a while to get back to sleep. I had one thing on my mind: Todd.

He was coming today. I had thought a lot about seeing him, and the day was here. My mind raced. What would it be like? Would I have the guts to say how I really felt? Would I feel differently about him? Could I tell him what was really on my mind, really tell him, to his face? What would he think of me then? Would he leave? Would it be over? Would he no longer be my friend, no longer my life coach?

What would he look like? What would he wear? Would I still be attracted to him? Had I built all this up in my mind? Should I hug him?

Of course. Yes, hug him.

I wanted to hug Todd. I missed him. I wanted to bridge the distance. I wanted to close the gap.

Maybe a hug was a bad idea? Maybe I shouldn't hug him? Maybe that would just make things worse? Okay, no hug. But I *wanted* to hug him. So, was I being inauthentic?

Oh, god. Enough!

I got out of bed and went to my laptop. Writing would help. My obsessive thoughts were out of control!

I had been avoiding writing about what was currently happening in my life. I hadn't written in almost two weeks. I didn't want to write about TJ or our marriage. I also didn't want to write about Todd. I was scared that he'd see right through me.

I started typing and quickly found myself back in late April, early May. Funny, I didn't *want* to write about Todd but that's exactly what I was doing.

I thought back to when I had shared with him about my brother's death, how I had felt about Todd then and being in the space of building trust. As my current thoughts about Todd started to blend and intertwine with how I'd felt about him before, I began to feel more at peace now and less anxious. I didn't feel as wrong.

I was lost in these thoughts when Lucy's black nose nudged my arm. Must be that time. Sure enough, 7:03 a.m. Time to run.

We ran a short loop. I ran strong. I was getting stronger, and running the loop was getting easier.

Although it was not a peaceful run, I still enjoyed being out there ... but I didn't get the high. My mind was racing, again.

The closer it got to 9:30 a.m., the more nervous I was. Should I tell Todd, or not, how I felt? I could bail on the idea, talk about something else, he would never know.

Yes, he would. He would know. Besides, I would never be free of this if I didn't tell him the truth. I must.

150

OPTING IN

I finished the run, took out the trash, cleaned the kitchen, emptied the dishwasher, ate cereal, took a shower, did a load of laundry, and vacuumed. Lucy followed me room to room, wondering what was going on with me.

I was running out of things to keep me busy. I decided to write. It was nine a.m. Lucy immediately fell asleep at my feet. I went back to May and read some of my notes from then. I couldn't believe what I was reading.

On May 2, I'd been feeling very anxious about my feelings toward men in certain relationships. I was very vague in the writing, but I could see now that I was writing about Todd. I'd been attracted to him even then, and that had scared the shit out of me. I had felt it then. I felt it now. Wow. There was no escape.

Just tell him, Molly. Be brave. Tell him.

He knocked. I walked around the corner to the living room and saw him outside through the beveled glass in the front door. My heart raced.

I opened the door, and Lucy wanted to meet him first to see if he was an acceptable stranger to come inside. Todd started petting her and immediately she was in love. It never takes much.

Todd was so at ease. I was anxious and uncomfortable.

I gave him a quick hug. No magic spark, just a hug. How simple that was, and I'd made such a big deal out of it.

"Well, shall we sit down and start?" he asked nonchalantly.

"Sure." I offered him a seat at the dining room table where I had been writing.

151

"So, how are you?" he asked.

My time was up. No more stalling. I started explaining, in very vague terms, how I felt when I was in a cycle of obsessive behavior.

"So is this about TJ?" he asked.

Deep breath. "No. It's about you."

"Me?"

"Yeah."

"Again?"

"Yes ... you."

I looked right into Todd's eyes. I told him how I had been obsessing about him, what he said and did, how I'd made everything mean something about him. If he called, that meant something. If he didn't call, that meant something. If he e-mailed, that meant something. If he didn't e-mail, that meant something.

I took a second, then added, "Todd, I'm attracted to you. I have feelings for you ... and I feel wrong for feeling this way. I'm married, you're married, and you're my coach. I shouldn't feel this way, and it's causing me anxiety and upset, but I don't know how to stop it. I don't know what to do with it. I haven't told you, because I was afraid you wouldn't coach me anymore, that you would leave."

I took a breath. "But I want to be able to always tell you what's on my mind." He just looked at me. I stared at the table and said, "This is so awkward."

He smiled. "You're doing great."

What I heard was, *You can trust me.* I felt better. In just calling a spade a spade, in just saying what was, I felt free. A weight lifted, and the maddening thoughts stopped.

"Why do you think you're wrong for these thoughts?" he asked.

I looked at him kind of funny.

He continued, "I have crushes on several women—but I don't act on those feelings, and I don't feel wrong for the thoughts."

He had crushes on other women? That made me feel better. If Todd had similar thoughts, maybe there wasn't something wrong with me, after all? Maybe it was *okay* to have these thoughts?

Again he asked, "Why do you think the thoughts are wrong? They are just thoughts."

I thought for another moment. "I've always felt a huge inconsistency between my thoughts and my actions. If society says it's wrong to kill, why is thinking about killing not wrong? If it's not okay to sleep with someone else when you're married, why is it okay to think about it? If we call an action wrong, why isn't the thought wrong?"

I continued: "I have felt that if I think one thing and do another, I'm not being honest, I'm not being authentic. I've tried to be a person of integrity my whole life. I've always tried to do the right thing. But I have thoughts all the time that are inconsistent with that. I'm married and I've been faithful, but I think about other men, or another man." I blushed. "I think that's wrong," I continued. "I want to live by integrity more than anything. The dichotomy is ripping me apart, creating a madness in my mind."

Todd said, "I have a choice. Thoughts come and thoughts go. I don't have control over them. However, I can control what I do with them. I can control my actions."

I thought about that. I heard what he was saying. I could continue making my thoughts wrong and suffer, or I could accept my thoughts and choose how to respond to them.

Then Todd surprised me. "You know, Molly, I feel the same way."

I couldn't believe what he had just said. "What?"

"I have those same thoughts. I've thought about it, too. Does that make you feel better?"

Actually it did, a lot better. "Yes, it does." I'd been making myself feel like a terrible person, and Todd felt the same way. Wow.

I shook my head. "This is ridiculous."

"It doesn't have to be," he said.

I could see that Todd wasn't suffering over this, like I was. Suddenly, the whole thing felt funny. I was psyched—not that I would do anything about it, just psyched. Someone thought I was attractive. *Todd* thought I was attractive. That felt wonderful.

"What would you want in our relationship if there were no constraints from society?" Todd asked.

Interesting. I liked the question. I took a few minutes to think about it. I was attracted to Todd, but I knew the relationship would never be the same if things went further. The connection I felt to him was almost indescribable, and I wouldn't compromise that with anything, certainly not with sex.

I finally answered, "I would want what we have now, without feeling bad about it."

"You can always say what is so for you with me," he said.

I searched for the right words to how I felt then: close, intimate, affectionate. Love was close -- but not romantic love; instead, it was the love of another person's soul. With tears starting to form from the magnitude of the connection I felt in that moment, I looked Todd right in his eyes and said, "I love you."

He smiled. "I love you, too."

Our conversation then drifted, all over, wonderfully. It was amazing.

After Todd left, for the first time I felt okay. I didn't worry. I didn't analyze the conversation. I was happy. I was at peace.

CHAPTER 18
The Beauty in My Roller-Coaster Craziness

"The question is not what you look at, but what you see."
- Henry David Thoreau

The feeling of peace and happiness stayed with me. It was usually so fleeting. Something was different now. Something was settling in.

The next day when I went to work, I forgot my cell phone. No big deal, even though I had NEVER been without it before. It was always with me, even next to my bed. I also always constantly checked it. Any calls? Texts? E-mails? Check, check, check.

Today, I didn't go back for it—and I actually liked how I felt without it. Free. I could let my thoughts go. It was a very unusual feeling.

I felt calm, content, relaxed. Life slowed down. I was still busy—but my mind was slower. I wasn't anxious or panicky. I wasn't obsessing. I just was.

I had a few great days. One morning, I had been writing for an hour before it even occurred to me that I hadn't checked my phone. I hadn't checked to see if Todd had e-mailed. The thought hadn't even crossed my mind.

This is good. This is very good.

I thought back on my relationship with Todd. Up, down; high, low … mostly low. I had tortured myself a lot, mostly over how I thought he felt about me.

The roller-coaster ride about Todd certainly was not the only one. Colin, that was a wild ride! Even the job. I had gone from loving it to hating it to loving it again. I had quit and gone back.

My marriage with TJ was certainly a tough ride. But I'd held on, confronted myself, and addressed it, fairly. *Then* realized I was still in love with him. Wow. How crazy is that?

I began to see the beauty in my roller-coaster craziness. In each event, I had learned I had a choice. I could stay down and agonize—blaming, reacting, avoiding responsibility. Or I could climb up.

My way out had been telling the truth. This had freed me from my mental spiral downward.

As I wrote my thoughts, I noticed a folder on my computer with a bunch of notes for the book. The folder had been on my computer desktop for ages. I'd forgotten about it. Today was a good day to clean it out, delete what no longer fit me.

I came upon a file with a strange name: C1. It was a letter I had written to Colin a long time ago—but had never sent. The date astonished me. I had written it exactly one year ago today.

Colin, there are a lot of things I don't know. I'm not a doctor, lawyer, CEO, or a surgeon. But I do have loyalty, integrity, and a huge heart. When I tell you I'm going to do something, I do it.

When I shook your hand when we decided to start this business, it was a lifetime deal. I'm in it for the long haul. I would never leave you or the company in a bad way. That is just not how I operate.

I came back to work because I came back for you. I gave you my word and I'm honoring it. As much as I am a part of this company, I want to be a part of your life. I want you to continue to be a part of my life. I want us to be friends, not a word I use lightly.

I would like to hang out with you. Go hiking, skiing, walking, or whatever. I want to be able to call you without a reason, just to say hi. I want your friendship.

I guess what I'm asking is, can we be family? Can you be my brother? Will you be a part of my life? Can we be more than just business? I hope so.

As I reread my own ramblings to myself, I was glad I hadn't sent it. It was more for me than for him. I had wanted to keep him in my life, but didn't know how to say it.

The most surprising aspect of this letter was that it was a wish list and, now, it was true. Colin was my friend and my old infatuation was behind me. I was very content with what we had now.

In this last year, through my deep self-reflections, as agonizing as they had been, I had grown. I now knew how to be a friend and not cling to a fantasy.

To actually create what you want in your life is indescribable. You realize that anything is possible. Such joy and energy fill you that grace embraces you and you feel fully present. That is magical!

The recent weeks with Colin had been magical. How wonderful to be his friend. I could open my heart and let him in. I could share my regrets and shame. The funny thing is, I no longer had regrets. I was no longer burdened by the shadows of my past.

Colin also had let me in. He had told me about his family, about growing up, what he loved to do, his passions. Funny, one of his passions was fishing. All the men in my life had loved to fish.

The best part of our new friendship was that I felt a love for Colin from that deep place where we really treasure another human being.

What was really curious was that I had read this old letter now that we *were* friends, in the same way that I had read about my earlier feelings for Todd before we had our new understanding. This had even happened with TJ.

It was like some part of me was dredging up the past so I could see it from a new perspective. Some part of myself was guiding me. Each time was a shift into a new reflection of myself, the self I was becoming.

This reminded me of those old 3D pictures where all you see is a bunch of dots. When you look at it a certain way, the 3D image pops out. Up to this point, my life had been a bunch of dots.

Now, for the first time, I saw the picture of my life and I couldn't go back. I had a new image—of myself—and nothing had really changed except me.

For the first time, I could see myself from the outside and the inside, and I finally got that there had been nothing wrong with me; there was nothing to fix. My unhappiness wasn't from a lack of something. I'd had all the pieces all along. They'd just never fit together before.

Todd had helped me to see my picture in the dots, that there was something greater about me than all my dots, that my whole being was breathtaking.

OPTING IN

The next morning, I took Lucy for a walk. It had snowed overnight. I usually dreaded the first snow and would begin counting the days back to spring. I always got cold easily and the winter months seemed to go on longer and longer. It was like my entire body rejected winter.

However, now I welcomed the snow! I marveled at the beauty of the freshly blanketed earth. Everything was so peaceful and clean. I could have stayed out all day and never felt cold.

The snow continued to fall. Overnight, it turned to ice. I had to scrape the ice off my car windows before going to work, but I enjoyed it! Unbelievable!

All week, I put on my running gear and headed out at seven a.m. It didn't matter if it was snowing or freezing. I couldn't wait to go out. It didn't bother me that it was dark and icy. I welcomed it! I saw something new in each thing I used to loathe. The world looked different. Everything took on a whole new meaning.

As the days rolled on, I woke up happy each morning. The high had never lasted before. This was new.

I kept expecting the crash to come, but it never did. I kept thinking I would wake up one morning and see only dots, but each new day my new life still remained. I couldn't *unsee* it. Just as a butterfly cannot crawl back into its cocoon, I could not undo the shift that had occurred inside me.

CHAPTER 19
The Deep Within

"Love seems the swiftest but it is the slowest of all growths.
No man or woman really knows what perfect love is until they
have been married a quarter of a century." - Mark Twain

The next day, TJ came back into town and was going to be around for a couple of days—and I looked forward to seeing him. We had been talking on the phone and I was enjoying our talks. I was interested in our conversations, interested in *him*.

I was excited to have dinner with TJ at our house and spend time together, although I was anxious about how I would feel. Would the old spark be there? Would our time apart have changed things? How would it go? How would we feel about each other? Could we work things out? Would I want to?

It didn't go well. I walked into a storm. I had expectations about everything, and none of it bore out. I had expected to feel closer to TJ, expected the evening to be fun and exciting. I had expected him to be more independent and energized than he used to be. I had expected to feel at ease and full of joy. I felt none of this.

As we sat for dinner at our dining table, I could feel my mood changing. I had been on a high all day at work and I came home to find TJ had cooked a beautiful dinner ... and it felt like he was walking on eggshells around me. My old feelings began to creep back in, and I felt guilty. Not where I wanted to be.

I hadn't seen TJ in weeks, but the first thought that came to mind was *He is too good for me.* I saw how much effort he had put into making this dinner for me, and I felt like shit. I hadn't done anything for him. Why? I asked myself.

As we started to eat, I began to feel irritated and I didn't know why. I tried to push it out of my mind.

Immediately, TJ started scraping his teeth on his fork, a habit of his. I couldn't stand it. I tried to go with it. I tried to rise above it. It got louder and louder. I was right back to the squeaking bike. I didn't want to feel this way. What was wrong with me?

This was the inevitable crash. Down the rabbit hole again. Peace and happiness gone.

As our conversation continued, I spiraled further and further down. I could *not* do this! I could not stay married. TJ and I were finished! I could not live with feeling irritated and vexed all the time.

I distanced myself as we sat there, in our old roles. The more we talked, the worse I felt.

Finally, I stood. "I can't do this. I'm going to bed."

"But it's only eight o'clock? We'll find common ground," he said meekly.

"It will just get worse," I mumbled.

I said goodnight and went to brush my teeth. He followed, right into the bathroom, and started brushing his own teeth.

"Are you kidding me?" I walked out to the other bathroom.

"Oh, am I bothering you?" he said.

"You've been bothering me all night! I really want some space."

"How can we get anywhere in this relationship if you keep wanting space?" he countered.

"This is not going to fix itself overnight. Be patient," I pleaded. "I need space right now."

"We just need to talk this out. Let's not go to bed mad," he reasoned.

I understood his point. We had always agreed not to go to bed mad. I just couldn't do that anymore. I couldn't have this same conversation *again*. I didn't want to talk any more, not one more minute.

"I can't," I said and walked into our bedroom and closed the door behind me, not waiting for his response.

I turned off the light and crawled into bed. I closed my eyes and it felt good to lie in the darkness.

The door opened. "Molly, can we please talk about this?" TJ walked in and sat on the bed.

I sat up immediately. "You are not listening to me," I said furiously. "You are not *getting* me. You have to go."

He huffed out of the room.

So, I'm the bad guy?

I did feel guilty. That was the problem. I was always feeling guilty.

We had agreed on how this evening would go. He would come over and we would make dinner together. It didn't happen.

Also, I had told TJ I wasn't ready to sleep in the same bed, and we had agreed that he would spend the night in the spare bedroom. Agreed. So why was I the jerk for kicking him out of the bedroom?

The tears started. Oh, my god. I couldn't be happy for five minutes?

More discouraged than ever, even so I didn't roll over to cry myself to sleep. I would not go there. I got up and, again, shut the door.

I went inside my walk-in closet and scrunched in a corner under my jeans that hung above me. In the dark, on my cell phone, I dialed Todd, not for a shoulder to cry on, not just to pacify me. I needed the truth, and I knew I could count on Todd for that.

His phone rang several times. Voicemail answered. I was *not* devastated.

"Hey," I said, "TJ came over tonight and it didn't go well. I'll call you later."

I hung up and went back to bed. Leaving the message—connecting—was all I had needed. I fell asleep quickly, but woke several times throughout the night. The heat had been turned up and I was way too hot. In frustration. I got up and took Advil. I had a terrible headache. I went back to bed and woke again at three a.m. I finally got up at five.

I wouldn't write today. Nothing good could come of my foul mood. I logged onto the internet to check my e-mail, and realized that my headache was gone and I *did* feel like writing. So, I'd give it a shot.

Before I knew it, an hour had passed and I had written some great material.

Wait a second. I thought I was down the rabbit hole? Guess not! Happiness had anchored deep within me. Cool.

I prepared to send Todd my writing for the day, our agreement to keep me accountable. Wait a second. Ever since I'd left the phone message, I hadn't thought much more about it. I hadn't spent the night obsessing. Instead, my creative spirit had inspired me. A nice change.

I e-mailed Todd about how TJ had come home and I'd had expectations that didn't bear out, *and* how I had *not* cried over it. I hit *send*.

In that instant, Todd called.

"Wow, I just sent you an e-mail, a short one," I said.

"You sound better."

"I am." I grinned. "I felt sad last night, but I'm okay now. It's going to be a good day."

Todd was psyched for me. Me, too.

With TJ still asleep in the spare bedroom, I grabbed Lucy and headed out for the run. It turned out to be a great run in the snow and ice. I had a huge grin on my face as I ran in the cold air and enjoyed every minute of the five miles. I was running in the present, a perfect start to the day, energized and inspired.

I came back from the run almost as excited as Lucy. We bounded in the door. TJ was up and making coffee.

"I'm sorry about last night," he apologized.

"Me, too," I said, realizing that I really was.

167

"Let's start over," we both said at the same time.

We both laughed and the lightness in the air was a stark contrast to the heaviness just twelve hours before.

TJ was headed to Denver to participate in the Landmark Forum. We talked about it before he left. He shared his excitement and trepidation. I told him there might be an opportunity for him to call me during the weekend and to feel free to do so. I wanted to hold that space for him to share, if he wished, without worrying about our agreement to give each other space.

I was excited for TJ and cautious not to create more expectations for what he should get out of his participation in the forum. I just had a feeling that it would have a profound impact on his life and mine. I was cautiously optimistic.

Todd and I had agreed to talk again at nine when we both had more time.

"I thought I was down the rabbit hole again," I said, "but I wasn't! I feel great. It's like a film has been lifted. Like I was looking through dirty glasses and now they're crystal clear."

As our conversation wound down, I wanted to talk about *us*. We had said a lot of things the last time we saw each other, and I wanted to check in with how we were both feeling now about it. And just like that, Todd brought it up. Cool. We were so in-sync.

"So, how are you feeling about us?" he said.

I grinned. "I feel free from my madness. The awkward attraction feeling is gone. It's more of a pure love."

"Yes, it's a sibling love," he said.

"Exactly."

I loved how Todd could say what I was struggling to express. He understood me. He got me.

This was the piece missing with TJ. He didn't get me. Anything but. We were in a vicious cycle.

He was always putting me first. The more he did, the guiltier I felt for not giving him more. It was like he got to be righteous and I got to be the jerk. I was tired of feeling bad.

For weeks, I constantly got the same questions from my brother Lee, from Colin, from Todd. "What is happening with you and TJ? What are you going to do?"

My answer: "I don't know."

I knew I loved TJ, and I wasn't ready to walk away from him. I loved him in a way I never had with anyone else. He was my rock, my one and only, the one man I knew would never leave my side. And I did hold a special place in my heart for him, a place very sacred.

After my older brother Ben had died, I had sought the bond I had with him in every male relationship. Out of all the men I had known, only one had made me feel special: TJ. Now I feared he would leave me, or I would drive him away.

So, why did I feel worse when he was nicer to me? Why was I meaner to him? Why did I resist the very thing I wanted?

I had changed. Maybe I no longer needed protecting?

The truth is, I wanted TJ to change, too. I wanted him to be more independent, like when I'd first met him. I didn't want him to cater to my every need. I didn't want him walking on eggshells around me. I wanted him to step up and be a man, to call me on my shit.

I also knew I didn't want to venture out on my own and leave TJ behind. I wanted him to fly with me. I wanted us to soar together.

CHAPTER 20
One Step at a Time

"The greatest step is out the door." - German proverb

I had been training for months and it was time. Time to run. For my first half marathon I wanted two things: for the course to be flat, and the temperature to be warm. I got neither.

I had signed up in advance for the Valley of Fire Half Marathon outside of Las Vegas, Nevada. I thought anything around Vegas would be both flat and warm. I was wrong on both counts. The one time I didn't do my homework, I would really pay for it.

TJ and I had talked about the race at length and both agreed it would be fun for him to come along. He had been instrumental in my training schedule and he wanted to be there with me. I was ready to have him there, too, and to spend some real time together.

Our conversations had improved immensely and we were enjoying each other. This was a huge step after our dinner breakdown. Driving to Las Vegas was the perfect time to test the waters with TJ, to see if we could still have a relationship.

We had hours of car time on each end of the trip to talk, catch up, and start to answer some of the questions about *us*. I was excited about this opportunity to test our relationship, but also nervous. I wanted to move forward in the marriage, but I was full of fear. What if things ended up like the last time, with TJ angry and me hiding in the closet? There was only one way to find out. Jump in.

The disaster started before I even stepped into the car to drive the ten hours to the outskirts of Vegas. This time, it wasn't TJ. I had planned on leaving at noon. I usually worked a half day on Fridays, which was perfect to get a jump on the trip early. However, on Friday morning when I walked into work, everything that could go wrong did. In addition to a new mountain of paperwork on my desk, two expensive pieces of medical equipment broke simultaneously and needed replacing, and one of our computer servers had gotten a virus overnight. Then, a four-year-old spilled food all over the waiting room and when I went to clean it up, the vacuum spit out dirt instead of sucking it up. Even more troubling, a long-term employee wasn't working out and I had to fire her, today.

It was close to three in the afternoon before I finally could leave the office. TJ picked me up at work. Our Subaru Outback was packed. Lucy was curled up in the back.

With three hours behind our travel schedule, the whiny voice in my head screamed at me to quit the race. I thought about all the work I had not gotten done, and I broke down in tears.

After several minutes of me wailing, TJ said supportively, "Molly, just bail."

I sniffed and mustered, "I don't want to let everyone down."

"It's just a race. You don't have to beat yourself up about it."

"I committed to this race. I gave my word. I always go 90 percent of the way with something, then quit. Not this time. I'm doing this. I can't let myself down."

So, TJ started the car and we headed along the winding mountain roads toward the desert. However, my tears continued to flow. *I can't win,* I whined to myself. *I'm letting the office down. I'm letting Colin down.*

If I didn't go, however, I would be letting myself down. I would be letting TJ down, Todd down, Lucy down. I wouldn't be honoring my word.

TJ looked over at me patiently. "What do you want to do?"

"Take one step at a time," I answered, from my wise self somewhere inside.

"What about the race?"

"I am so not ready."

"Just take one step at a time," he repeated back to me.

I grinned. "Got it. One step at a time."

I took a few deep breaths, and I actually began to feel good, even excited.

"What just happened?" I said out loud. "A breakdown like this used to last weeks."

TJ smiled at me. "You *are* fine ... and that is so not normal."

"I know."

"You were so upset just a few minutes ago. Before, that would have ruined your weekend."

I shook my head. "It's amazing to me, too."

"That Landmark stuff must work."

"Well, something is. I sure feel better."

He smiled.

"I guess I have finally figured out, I get to *choose* how I'm going to feel." I smiled confidently. "No more playing victim for me. And when I walk into the office on Monday, I will tackle one thing at a time."

TJ nodded. "That's all anyone can do."

I grinned. "Yeah, trying to do ten things at once was getting me nowhere." Then I realized, "Shit, I'm running a half marathon. I'm not a distance runner. I convinced myself I'm up to it, but I don't think my body can handle more than six to ten miles, not thirteen. What was I thinking? I can't run a half marathon. Oh, crap. What have I done?"

TJ just looked over at me. "One step at a time" was all he said.

I nodded. *Right.*

We got into town late and checked into our hotel after midnight. TJ and I had talked about the logistics of coming on this trip together. He had wanted to come. I had wanted it, too. I didn't know our future, but right now I wanted to be with him.

We got one hotel room with separate beds. It was silly to get two rooms. Also, logic aside, I wanted him close.

Going from being irritated, annoyed, and frustrated with TJ to enjoying and looking forward to his company was a huge change. To my surprise, I was happy with him and our conversations were better than ever. We were both really listening and *hearing* each other.

I still didn't know if the spark would return, the butterflies. Would I adore him again? But we were building a friendship, and I felt we were on a solid footing.

I fell asleep quickly and slept hard until three a.m. Then I lay awake worrying about the race. At five a.m., it was time to get up and go to the Valley of Fire.

I always ran better on an empty stomach, so we skipped breakfast. My stomach was a mess anyway, cramping like crazy from nerves.

As we drove to the Valley of Fire State Park, my nervousness intensified. "I really thought I would be okay with this race and just enjoy it," I muttered.

"You are going to be amazing," said TJ.

"I want to believe you," I said bravely.

As we pulled into a parking space, he pointed. "There's a Port-a-Potty."

I raced to it. What a horrible smell!

Just as I shut the door, I heard the announcement that everyone should line up for the race, and there I was on the toilet. Diarrhea, my prerace ritual.

I finally opened the door. TJ was holding my jacket, my race packet, and a Gatorade for after the race. A little piece of me fell in love with him, again.

I was running, stress behind me, ticking off the miles.

I missed my running companion. Lucy was at home with friends, since dogs are not allowed in the park. She had been with me on every training run, and it just didn't feel right not to have her here with me today.

I rounded the first corner and stared straight up at the first of many huge hills, not flat at all, not even close. Huge rolling hills, up, down, then right back up.

The first six miles, I felt strong and I ran hard, and no one was passing me. I didn't even stop at any of the aid stations. I rocked!

By mile eight, however, I realized that gale force winds had been at my back. I'd had it easy.

I paid for that advantage in the last five miles, which were brutal: never-ending hills and the wind against me in my face, like I was going nowhere.

At one point, I looked up and saw everyone around me walking, just walking. I was about to slow down, too, when Todd's last words came to me: "Molly, kick ass."

So, I ran. Every hill. Over, and over, and over. Kick ass! Kick ass! Kick ass!

At the crest of the final hill, I saw the \spectators cheering and my heart lifted. I picked up my pace and flew down the steep decline. What a rush!

The last few feet, the cheering grew louder, people clapping, ringing cowbells, yelling for *me*, and photographers snapping pictures. I was a celebrity!

I dashed across the finish line, and there was TJ—with the most amazing smile and I was so glad to see him!

I collected my medal (one given to everyone for finishing the race) and hurried through the crowd to him.

"I did it!" I screamed.

He gathered me up in a bear hug and I embraced him with my whole being. I was so glad he was there!

CHAPTER 21
Another Barrier Down

"No person was ever honored for what he received. Honor has been the rewards for what he gave." - Calvin Coolidge

Driving back from Vegas afforded plenty of quality and long-overdue talk time with TJ. However, I didn't want to talk about the marriage now. I didn't even want to think about it.

Eventually, he looked over and tentatively asked me, "What's the plan? What are we going to do?"

I hesitated. "I don't know. The truth is -- I'm scared."

"Scared of what?"

I looked down. "Scared that it will be like it was."

We continued to drive in silence and I pondered: What was I afraid of?

I was afraid of going backward, I admitted to myself. I had been so unhappy. I didn't want to lose what I now had. I had worked so hard to get here. So I had no idea how we could move forward.

TJ must have been thinking the same thing. "I want to work with a coach," he suddenly announced.

"Wow. What makes you say that?" I asked, shocked.

"I can see that Todd has helped you. I want that for me, too ... and for us." He paused. "I'll do whatever it takes, Molly."

"I think it's a great idea. Let's find you a coach."

"I already have one in mind."

"Really? Who?'

"Todd."

My heart raced at the mere suggestion. Todd? Actually, Todd and I had talked before about how a coach could help TJ. However, I had never envisioned it would be *my* coach. Wasn't that a conflict of interest? Todd *could* help TJ, but I didn't *want* him to coach both me *and* my husband. Plus, I wanted *Todd* to be the one to say it was not a good idea.

I finally responded. "Well, it's certainly something to think about."

We left it at that. There was a lot left unsaid.

A couple of days later, the subject still loomed in the air. I briefly talked with Todd about it, and voiced my concern about Todd's coaching both of us. I was relieved when Todd said he would find a coach for TJ.

A week or so later, Todd relayed that the other coach wondered why Todd wasn't coaching TJ himself. My heart fluttered. I could see where this was going. Yes, Todd and his colleague had both agreed that Todd was, in fact, the perfect coach for TJ.

I stammered, "I thought we decided this already, that you weren't going to coach TJ?"

There was silence on the other end of the phone. Todd finally said, "I've thought a lot about it, and I really think I can help you *both*. I want to do this. I want to coach TJ."

I felt myself sliding down the rabbit hole. I thought Todd was coaching me because he cared about me. The instant he said he *wanted* to coach TJ, I realized I was a client, period.

This would change everything. There would be no more privacy. What about confidentiality? Wouldn't I lose my special connection with Todd?

Todd had looked out for me. I had felt a sense of security. What now? I had thought he was on my team, like a big brother looking out for me. I didn't want that to change.

No!

I felt my special connection to Todd slipping away. He would no longer be in my court. He couldn't.

Feelings of abandonment rushed through me, and I realized I did feel like a sister to Todd. Now I was losing another brother.

My walls and defenses had been down with Todd. How could I ever be as open with him again? He had shown me how to be strong, how to believe in myself. What would I do now?

As all of these thoughts raced through my mind, Todd asked, "Are you worried that TJ will tell me something you don't want me to know?"

I didn't know whether to laugh or cry. I was more worried about not being special. In that instant, things were different between us. Todd didn't get it. He didn't get me.

I felt anger building. "You think TJ may tell you something I don't want you to know? I have only been honest with you both. So, it doesn't matter what you say to each other."

Why was it selfish to want my own coach? What if Todd coaching TJ altered my relationship with TJ for the worse?

Yet despite my fear and guilt, I thought of TJ. He was asking for a coach. He was fighting for our marriage, for me, for himself—and I wanted this for him.

So, for the first time in a *very* long time, I put my own desires aside and did what I thought was best for TJ. I didn't feel it was best for me, but it was for him.

After my talk with Todd, I found TJ. "Yes, absolutely, Todd will coach you. It will be amazing for you."

Then, suddenly, something settled in me. Something became very clear. What did I have to fear? What was happening was *exactly* what needed to happen. Todd coaching TJ was exactly how it needed to be. I felt aligned. I stopped arguing with myself. This was the best, for everyone, including me.

"Aren't you concerned?" asked TJ.

"If this is what you want, then I want this for you, too."

He smiled. "You've changed a lot."

I smiled. "I'm still working on it."

"I know — that's why it means so much."

Suddenly I felt so close to him. A barrier had fallen.

"I know it's not easy," he said.

I nodded. "Life happens as it happens. It's perfect."

"That's what I love about you, Molly."

I just looked deeply into TJ's eyes. There was the man with whom I had fallen in love.

I also got the absurdity of thinking that Todd viewed me only as a client. I worked for Colin. Did I do it only for the money? No, I did it because he was a friend. Todd and I were friends. We couldn't open up, and he couldn't go to the deep place with me, if he wasn't really my friend. I laughed.

"What's so funny?" said TJ.

"I still like to make myself crazy. You know how my thoughts go on and on."

"You are worried."

I nodded. "I'm still learning how not ... not to be afraid. But, TJ, it's time. Maybe Todd coaching you will help us in our marriage, and I do want that."

"Do you?"

"Yes. I want it to be better between us. *I* want to be better."

"I'm glad. For a while there, I wasn't sure."

"Me, either ... but I am now. No more half in or half out. No more sitting on the fence."

I owned the moment, choosing the marriage. I wanted to be with TJ. I was fully committed, fully on board.

The weight of this commitment suddenly struck me. How could I create a happy marriage when I was in so much fear?

Take the first step, Molly, said my wise inner voice. *One step at a time.*

CHAPTER 22
No More Running Away

"All great changes are preceded by chaos." - Deepak Chopra

Early one workday morning, TJ was lying on the couch. He didn't look good.

"Are you okay?" I asked.

He simply said, "No … I might need to go to the emergency room."

This was so unlike him. I could barely get him to go to any doctor, and he was suggesting the ER?

I calculated my day. If we left now, I could make it to work and be close to being on time. Many unresolved fiascos in the office, from before my half marathon run in Vegas, still needed to be fixed. I felt under water. Plus, this week was Thanksgiving, our busiest week of the year, and we were already overbooked.

I cringed with guilt. I was thinking about my job when TJ had just told me he needed to go to the ER.

"I know how much you have to do today," he apologized, as if reading my mind. "I'll be okay. It's just a stomachache. If it gets worse, I promise, I'll call you."

I had a choice. I could stay home and take care of TJ, or go to work. I chose work. Yes, the job. I had criticized my mother for this very same choice. Once, I hadn't talked to her for two weeks when I had needed to go to the ER and she had chosen her job over me. Now, here I was doing the same thing.

At work, my mind was at home, worrying. Even so, it was noon before I realized I hadn't checked on TJ once. I fumed at myself. I was letting him down.

I called him and he had gone to a doctor. He was having spasms in his abdomen. The doctor had said it was nothing serious, and TJ said he was feeling better. Still, I felt badly that I hadn't put TJ first.

At the end of the day, over dinner, he still wasn't feeling good. We sat on the couch together and watched Monday Night Football: the Denver Broncos versus the San Diego Chargers. We rarely watched TV, so it was unusual to be doing this.

I felt an urge to go into my home office and write. However, I stayed with TJ and watched the game, trying to redeem myself for the morning.

Things went downhill. The Broncos once again embarrassed them-selves. As they fell apart against the Chargers, anger rose in me. Orton had the ball and the Broncos were finally working their way down the field. Progress! He threw a pass for the end zone, but it was beautifully intercepted.

"Damn it!" I yelled.

TJ cringed. "Why are you so angry? We're both tired. Let's just go to bed."

"No. I'm watching the rest of the game."

I no longer felt like being nice. The game didn't get any better. Neither did my attitude.

Several more times, TJ suggested we go to bed. I let the comments go and didn't answer. Just as the game was about over, TJ again suggested we go to bed.

"Stop telling me what to do!" I yelled. "If you're tired, then *you* go to bed. I'll go when I'm ready. God!"

He got up and left without a word.

Shit, I was meaner to him today than I'd been in months.

Still sleeping alone, I kept thinking about who I was when I was with TJ. I was so angry around him.

Why? I questioned.

I knew the answer. I was still afraid of dealing with the marriage ... because I wasn't sure how I really felt about him. Otherwise, why would I vacillate up and down so much?

Also, I could not avoid my obsessive worry. I really *didn't* want Todd to coach TJ. It was like bringing Todd into the marriage, bringing Todd into an area I had deemed off limits.

I had gotten to a good place with Todd. Now here I was again, obsessing over him: what he thought about me, how coaching TJ would change things.

I knew this was my old madness creeping back in—and I couldn't stop it. By opening up with Todd, things had moved in me. I had faced many fears and found peace. However, sharing my marriage with a third person, someone who knew all my secrets, gave him control over my life. I wanted to be in control of my own life.

In the middle of the night, lying there alone, once again I pushed Todd away. I would stop working with him. That was safer. If I left first, he couldn't leave me. So, once again, I shut him out. I shut down.

Come morning, I realized this was my pattern. I walked away first, always first, so I couldn't be abandoned.

Then I truly realized that I couldn't leave Todd. Things were going so well with me. I was in a much better place than ever before in my life.

You don't want to go down this road again, Molly, I told myself.

I didn't want to lose Todd! I liked him in my life. I must fight this. I must not walk away.

I sat down and wrote Todd an e-mail. It was embarrassing. Again, I asked if he cared about me. How many times had I been down this road? It was exhausting! Why did I keep doing this? It was ridiculous!

Yet, here I was doing it again. I told Todd how I was wanting to push him away, yet scared of losing him.

By the end of writing the e-mail, a new insight came to me. Something was different about me. My story was still old and tired—but my *behavior* was new. I was afraid, very—but I was not shutting down. I was *not* running away after all.

I sent the e-mail, feeling good.

Inexplicably, something still pulled at me. I still felt all jumbled up.

OPTING IN

Okay, Molly, I said to myself, *you can run and hide. You can stay stuck. Or you can be all in for the marriage to TJ. So, what's it going to be?*

"I'm all in!" I declared to myself.

TJ and I went to dinner to celebrate asking for Todd's help in our marriage. We went to the same restaurant where we'd had our huge breakdown last year. It did feel strange.

I thought about how my life could have ended that night. What if I hadn't gone to Landmark? What if I hadn't worked with Todd? What if I had run away? What if I had killed myself, after all?

I grinned. It had been the hardest year of my life—and the absolute best. I wouldn't change a thing.

Dinner went well, no tears. I made it through the entire evening without a meltdown. I even had fun with TJ. We talked and joked as we enjoyed our food. Nothing profound happened. It was a nice change.

Toward the end of the meal, the conversation turned to TJ's dad. Despite his brief spurt of enthusiasm for life after his open-heart surgery, he was in hospice now and not expected to make it through the weekend.

"Do you want to fly back to Ohio to be with him?" I asked.

TJ shook his head. "No, I'm at peace with him now. I told him I love him, and I just spent a week with him at the hospital."

I shared my story of recently telling my own dad that I loved him.

TJ smiled. "Okay, when we get home, I'll call my dad and tell him again how much I love him."

187

Through my journey this last year, TJ had been inspired through his own self-reflections. Looking into his eyes now, I could see that his recent week with his dad had been healing. Here was the man I loved.

I found you.

CHAPTER 23
My Icky Behavior

"So, instead of wanting to throttle your loved ones when they give you a hard time, it is better to look at them as mirrors of what you still need to work on in terms of your personal growth." - Susan Jeffers, *Feel the Fear...And Do It Anyway*

I met Todd at a Chinese restaurant after he finished his first coaching session with TJ. It was two in the afternoon and this was his first chance to get some lunch. When I walked in, he was already eating.

Todd didn't say much during this visit. He didn't have to. I couldn't help but notice the way he ate. He scraped his teeth with his fork, TJ's habit, which had almost ended our marriage.

My father had been so strict at the dinner table that I had been overly sensitive ever since. I couldn't stand the sound of teeth scraping! Todd did it, too? How weird.

At least TJ was learning to hardly do it anymore, because, once he did, I no longer listened to a word he said.

Todd's teeth scraping, however, was in a league all his own, like he knew it was a trigger for me. Of course, he didn't.

As I watched him eat, I realized, *Todd is not perfect*. He had once told me that he leaves honey all over the kitchen counter and that he farts. Neither of these had killed the fantasy for me. Now, however, I was beginning to get it. He had faults. Just as I had trouble with TJ, so I would in a relationship with Todd or anyone else. Oh.

Suddenly, my complaints about TJ seemed preposterous. I had been seeking perfection—in TJ, in the marriage, in my life ... in myself. Clearly, unrealistic. I certainly was not perfect.

Suddenly, I was excited to see TJ. I wanted to apologize, hug him, kiss him ... and have him sleep next to me.

As Todd and I left the restaurant, even though he wasn't perfect, I still thought he was one of the most attractive men I had ever met. He would always have a special place in my heart, teeth scraping and all.

I thought about TJ the rest of the day. I wanted his arms around me. I missed him.

The moment I walked through the door, I gave him a big hug, to his surprise. It had been a long time. I held him, held on to him, feeling again the love I had once felt.

I told TJ my new realization about my unrealistic expectations of him, the marriage, and myself, and relief washed over his face. A weight lifted from him.

"I'm sorry," I apologized. "You never had a chance."

He smiled and hugged me. "But now I do ... we do."

For the first time, there was lightness in our conversation. I was so glad! How wonderful this felt. We laughed, we joked.

"I've missed this," I said, my eyes teary.

"Me, too."

My heart warmed. Here was the man I had married.

For days, I felt like a teenager in love, giddy and excited to be around TJ. I couldn't get enough of him. I would open my eyes and he'd be the first thing I saw in the morning. It felt so right, so familiar. He belonged there, beside me.

Then there was the late-night phone call. TJ's phone, 11:00 p.m., his brother. Their dad had just passed away. He had fallen asleep and simply stopped breathing.

TJ was very quiet as he crawled back into bed. I held him for a long time and we didn't say anything. Memories of losing my own brother came back to me. The most comforting thing for me had been a hug. I held TJ until he fell asleep.

Over the next few days, TJ was in touch with his brothers and sisters, making arrangements, figuring out travel plans. I debated whether or not to go with him to Ohio.

I sat with the decision for a day, struggling with whether to go and support TJ or stay here and take care of my responsibilities at work. Finally, I said to TJ, "I want to go with you."

I saw a light in his eyes that had been missing. He couldn't believe I was going. That's when it became truly clear to me. I had a part in the breakdown of our marriage. I had checked out with TJ. I had been distant. I hadn't supported him or really listened to him in quite some time.

"Of course, I'll be there," I said.

At a time like this, you really do see who your friends are. Leaving work was not a problem, and TJ and I had several options for dog care. I felt so blessed. I hadn't felt blessed for many months. I had closed the door to my heart. I had shut people out. No more!

In Ohio on Friday morning, I woke at 6:30 a.m. next to TJ in the upstairs spare bedroom at his parents' house. I would have to wait until eight for my weekly call with Todd, which would be 6:00 a.m. in Colorado. I missed our habitual early call, when I always sat in the same place in my home office. It felt like *our* time.

I called Todd from the guest bedroom, where it was private, while TJ was downstairs with his family. I could picture Todd on his couch, with his earpiece, talking comfortably while the rest of his own family were still sleeping.

My conversation with Todd started out slow, even though he was upbeat as usual. Oddly, I was slightly on edge by his energy level and I realized I missed the quiet closeness of our chats before TJ had entered the picture.

I felt myself pulling away as I discussed how I was struggling to finish my book and how I was anxious to get it done.

Todd suggested that I take a break. "It's difficult to force the creative process," he said. "The best material usually doesn't come when you feel you *have* to do something."

I understood what he meant, but that was not what I wanted to hear. "But I don't want to take a break," I complained. "I want to finish this. Not only that, writing, like running, makes me happy, and I haven't been doing either. I miss the creative high, the energy rush. And I don't need you telling me to stop or slow down. No, that is not the answer."

I rambled on. "When I'm writing, or running, I discover magic. I'm in the moment. I'm present, like at no other time. I feel totally *me*. When I'm writing, I gain clarity. No, this is not the time to stop."

I was trying to convince myself, of course. I knew Todd had a point, but I didn't even want to consider it. He was just annoying me. This conversation was not going how *I* wanted it to go.

"So you're making a choice?" Todd said. "You're doing what you feel will make you happy, like your changes at your job?"

"That's just it. I get that we choose to be happy, but I think effort plays a role, too. Choosing to be happy can only get you so far. Effort is required for the higher steps."

"We can agree to disagree," was all Todd said.

"What does that mean?" I said belligerently, astonished at his response. Where was his empathy? I felt heat rise in my face. "You are draining all the inspiration out of me."

After a brief silence, Todd said, "Okay, let's take a look at that." He softened his tone. "Are you angry because I'm not agreeing with you?"

Busted. He saw right through me, and I hated that he could. I also was furious that he called me on this. So I justified myself. "You are so far off. You just don't get it," I fumed. "This is *not* about being right. You aren't *hearing* me. I don't want to agree to disagree. I want you to challenge my ideas and thoughts. Test me, push me, question me. But for godsake, not agree to disagree. That is so lame. Instead, help me understand *why* it works for you. I want to get it. Don't you see? I want to have this conversation."

Another very long silence on the phone. The conversation was spiraling down the toilet. This was so *not* how I wanted it to go.

So that was his attitude? He would believe his own way—the way that works—and I should do whatever works for me?

Bullshit. Fuck you, Todd. I thought you wanted to help me.

"I don't feel like you are very present right now," he said.

Great. Awesome.

Now he was insulting me because I didn't agree with him? *He* was the one not being present. Could he kick me any harder?

Full-on shut down.

I was present! *I* was in the moment … and thinking of nothing but Todd and this damn conversation.

Could I feel angry *and* be present? I questioned. *Am I present, or not?*

I took the easy road and just agreed with him. "You're right. I'm not being present."

"If you're not present, you can opt out of this conversation."

I flushed with shock. "What the hell now? Why would I want to opt out and hang up now?"

I didn't want to leave this. I wanted to talk it through. I wanted to feel better … and I wanted Todd to make me feel better.

"What if I want to opt out?" he said.

Everything in my mind stopped, and my heart raced.

What? Did he really say that? No. No. No.

The conversation in my mind started back up again. *Okay, Molly, stop and think. Why does Todd want to hang up?*

He no longer wants to talk to you at all, I answered.

This was bad. This was very bad.

I desperately needed Todd's attention. Why didn't he care about me? Wasn't I special to him?

The last thing in the world I wanted was for Todd not to want to talk to me. What happened? Why would he want to opt out?

I thought about that. It was true, I wasn't being nice to him. In fact, I was being short with him. This was not fun at all. And he was choosing out.

"What you are doing right now is not very attractive," Todd said as I spiraled downward. "When my son cries and throws a fit," he said, "and I go to him to see what's wrong, he has drawn me into his world. He wants my attention and, if I respond to his tantrum, he gets my attention. That's what you're doing, Molly, and it doesn't feel good."

The only thing I could think to say was, "If you want to opt out, that is your choice."

I would give him his space, but I was stunned.

I needed to think this over. Was it true? Was I acting like a five-year-old?

I *was* angry, and I *had* shut down. He was right, and I was mortified. I had just thrown a fit.

195

"You're right," I confessed.

"Okay, that's awesome. Now we're getting somewhere." Enthusiasm returned to his voice. "This is the most profound conversation we've had, Molly."

He was right. I thought back over my life. This icky, manipulating behavior of mine was like a cancer. I had shut down with Colin, shut him out of my life. I had shut down with my mom, dad, and friends. I had done it to all of them. In fact, only a handful of friends had remained in my life.

Talk about a blind spot. I'd never seen this in myself before. Now, the second I realized it, my anger toward Todd disappeared and I felt terrible for all the previous conversations he had endured. God, what he must think of me? Gross, really gross.

For the first time in my life, someone had stood up to me. Todd had called me on my shit. He had changed my life.

After the call, I sat in stunned silence. Was this who I was in the world? This did not make me feel proud—yet it was a major breakthrough. This knowledge about myself was the key to being the person I wanted to be. I could show up and be myself and love people without an agenda or needing anything in return. That was the kind of person who could do something big in the world, something that mattered.

I finally went to find TJ, excited to tell him about my breakthrough and to hear his thoughts. He was in his dad's living room, reading.

"How'd your talk go?" he asked.

Where to begin? "Well, it was interesting."

As I explained, a smile crept across TJ's face. By the time I was done, he was grinning ear to ear and laughing.

I smiled. "So this sounds familiar?"

He laughed even harder. "Um, yeah!"

"Wow. I really do this to you that often?"

"Molly, you do this to me all the time, constantly."

It didn't take long for me to realize he was right. I did play this controlling game with him. Wow. The magnitude of it hit me. He would do something I didn't like, then I would get angry with him and shut down. That generally meant being snippy, or I might not talk to him for a while. I had been punishing him for the slightest infractions, picking him apart, tearing him down. I had almost succeeded in ripping apart our marriage.

It was so clear now. It had never been about TJ. If he didn't do what I wanted, I'd get pissed. No matter what he did or didn't do, I was frustrated with him. If he made my lunch, he was needy; if he didn't, he was not being supportive. If he stayed around the house and did chores, he was not doing stuff in the world; if he went out and skied, he was being messy and not taking care of the house.

Imagine! I'd been at the point of walking away entirely. *He* was being himself and living *his* life. I had been manipulative and tried to control how he should live or I berated him. It was like he needed to read my mind, and when he didn't, game over.

How absurd of me! No wonder he was always walking on eggshells around me. How dare I! That wasn't the person I wanted to be.

This must have been awful for TJ. Why had he put up with me? Why did he stay with me through all of this? We had talked so many times about relationships where the man is dominating and controlling, and the woman does what he says and never complains. Yet that is exactly what I had been doing to our relationship.

I vowed to pay closer attention to being present and fair to TJ.

CHAPTER 24
Letting Love In

"Between stimulus and response there is a space. In that space
is our power to choose our response. In our response lies our
growth and our freedom." - Victor Frankl

The next day, we sat in the front row of the mass for TJ's father, next to his mother, his sister and her husband. TJ's brothers and sisters were crying. I could barely put myself in their shoes. I hadn't lost my father. The thought of it was too much even to imagine.

The priest talked about love, life, and loss. Although I wasn't religious myself, and was skeptical, his words left me in deep thought.

He said, "When we die, our tombstone has our name, our year of birth, a dash, and our year of death. That is all we are doing—living out the dash. In living out the dash we have two jobs. First, to love God. Second, to love our neighbors as ourselves."

Our *job* in life is to love? How well was I doing that? I wondered.

After my conversation with Todd, I now realized I'd been seeking love from people by being manipulative. Closing myself off when things didn't go my way was not loving my neighbors as myself; I didn't want other people doing that to me. Being courageous, loving full out, leaving nothing unsaid or undone—that would be being big in life.

Living out the dash of my life? Could I love with an open heart? Could I create a space for people to be open and honest with me about what is so for them? Could I do this without judging, without taking it personally, without getting my feelings hurt?

I thought of great people in the world like Martin Luther King Jr., Gandhi, Nelson Mandela. They had loved this way. They had listened and heard what others were saying, and look how they had shown up in the world. I wanted to love like that, in a *big* way.

First, I wasn't hitting the mark with an open heart; my heart had a double lock. How could I fix this? Make a few apologies, starting with Todd.

That night, I wrote Todd a real letter, using pen and paper. It would require a stamp.

> Todd, I would like to say thank you, and I'm sorry. You once told me that the stand you take for me is unwavering, period. I didn't fully understand the magnitude of your statement until our last conversation. No one has ever taken a stand for me like that before. I am truly moved. You have opened doors in my life. I will never be the same.
>
> Todd, I realize how I was behaving with you and I know how that feels. You were right. I have been seeking your attention and your respect, in a way that I know felt icky.
>
> It's shocking to know I have been doing this all my life, with everyone. I'm sorry. I want things to go a different way, especially with you. I love this journey and our work together.
>
> Again, thank you and I am sorry. I am inspired by your open heart. Todd, I love who you are being in the world. You are truly breathtaking.
>
> Molly

I also needed to apologize to TJ. He had taken the brunt of my frustrations and I finally understood how life had been for him.

He was in his parents' kitchen, holding a picture of his dad. He was just sitting there, staring. He looked up at me and I instantly felt like I had interrupted.

"I'm sorry," I quickly said.

"No, it's fine. I'm fine," he said quietly.

"I'll leave you alone," I said and began to retreat from the kitchen.

"No, please stay." He patted the chair next to him.

I sat and looked at him, and tears started to form in my eyes. "I'm really sorry."

"I told you, it's fine," he repeated.

"No, I don't just mean for that. I really am *sorry*. I'm sorry for everything." I started to cry, feeling the weight of it all. "I'm sorry, TJ, for being so mean to you. I'm sorry for not giving you a chance. I'm sorry for shutting down and shutting you out. TJ, I am so sorry."

"You never have to apologize to me," he said and reached his hand to me.

"I do. I *want* to. I want to apologize and tell you I finally get it. I get how awful I have been and I am so sorry."

"Molly, I love you. I will always love you. There is nothing you could do to ever change that," he said.

"You always say the right things. I'm stumbling over my thoughts and

201

words, and you say it just perfectly. I'm such a fuck-up."

"Yeah, but you're my fuck-up," he teased.

We both laughed and held each other, and I looked again into his eyes. "I'm not perfect, and I know I won't always get it right. I will fuck up ... and I will apologize." I smiled. "But I want you to know I do love you with my whole heart. You are the man for me, and I will spend the rest of my life showing you ... one day at a time."

"We're on this ride together, Molly ... always."

That was my thought exactly. Once again, he said it perfectly.

A week went by. TJ and I were back home in Colorado. The realization of my past behaviors continued to sink in. I paid attention whenever I felt agitated, frustrated, or annoyed. Then I would notice what was causing my reaction.

Often, just noticing was enough. Simply observing my emotions often seemed to diffuse the situation, as if just noticing that I was getting annoyed caused those feelings to go away.

It was shocking to notice how many times I felt frustrated and irritated. Incredible! Even more amazing was how fast these feelings could vanish when I saw them for what they were.

I thought back to college and all the great people I had left behind. I thought back further to high school, even earlier. I thought of my best friend and how I had let our friendship dissolve, how I see pictures of her son on Facebook and I deeply miss my friendship with her. I had tried to repair this friendship years ago, but now I could see I hadn't done it from an open heart.

OPTING IN

So many people had come in and out of my life. I had always thought they were leaving me. In fact, I had left them. I'd had it wrong all these years. I was the one who was always running away. I was always *running*.

The irony hit me one morning as I *was* running, with Lucy loping ahead on her leash.

"Still, I do love to run!" I shouted with joy to the world.

The saying "You can't judge in others what you don't see in yourself" also hit me, and I realized my behavior of shutting down and running away had been passive-aggressive. This shocked me, because I couldn't stand this behavior in others.

God! That was me? *I* was being the one thing I couldn't stand? Oh, my god.

I started laughing. I paused in my run and gave myself a minute to really guffaw. Lucy stopped and cocked her head at me, like what's so funny?

I laughed outrageously. "This is so hilarious! I'm nuts! Well, no more! No more fear of not being in control! I give it up! No more dictating the actions of my husband, my co-workers, my friends. I let it all go!"

I started running again, and Lucy danced ahead of me on the trail. I thought about the things I had feared: horses, roller coasters, planes, boats. Funny, all of them were things over which I had felt no control. It's funny when you look at your life and see yourself for just what you are.

"Got it!"

What if I had opted out?

I laughed. "But I didn't! And now I'm *really* here!"

I picked up speed in a joyous race up the hill, taking myself and my life to a higher level.

As I slowed to a walk to cool down on the way home, I thought of dearest TJ. He had never given up on me. He had persevered. The tougher I was on him, the more he had loved me. Wow. How lucky I was!

As I approached the house, I realized that the way I was feeling before—lost, unloved, out of control—didn't match the way the world saw me. I did feel the world loving me, but a war had been raging inside me. The outside world was bright, loving, and beautiful. Inside I had felt dark, alone, and ugly. With all of my breakthroughs, reading, the coaching, even the Landmark courses, the darkness had remained—until I realized I was fighting to *feel* loved, I was still feeling alone.

But no more. After my conversation with Todd, I now realized I had a choice.

When Lucy and I happily romped inside the house, I looked at TJ with a new heart. Instead of faults and imperfections, I saw a man who loved me as I was. He had loved me through it all. I now knew, at the core of my being, that I wanted TJ in my life forever. He was my friend, my lover, my life partner. I also knew everything would be okay now. I would be okay.

I hugged TJ and let him in. What a wonderful place to be.

CHAPTER 25
The Clear Knowing

Grandma: "You know, when I was nineteen, Grandpa took me on a roller coaster.... Up, down, up, down. Oh, what a ride! ... You know, it was just so interesting to me that a ride could make me so frightened, so scared, so sick, so excited, and so thrilled all together!" - *Parenthood, 1989*

Todd and I both agreed that I would take a month off from his coaching to give me time to discover what I wanted to do next with my life. I was still sorting that out.

It was time to fly on my own. Oddly, I was looking forward to the inevitable breakdowns and breakthroughs. How weird is that?

Quickly, I felt the familiar pressure of *I have to*, because I had to be up to something to work with Todd again, and I did want that.

Then just like that, I was strapped in and off on my roller-coaster ride— and loving it! My mind jerked me up and down as ideas worked their way to the foreground, trying to discover what I really wanted to do with my life.

The feeling of falling down the rabbit hole had been my companion for a long time. Thoughts of suicide had nagged at me since childhood.

Now I had an insight: What if I worked in suicide prevention? I had lived obsessively in the depths of the darkness, the despair, the loss of hope. I knew how it felt to feel so alone that you just want out.

I also realized that coaching and motivational speaking are important tools for helping people, and I truly wanted to share my stories about how I learned to live all-out and fully. By sharing my own breakdowns and breakthroughs, maybe I could help others learn for themselves how to stand up and be who they truly are, how to find and follow their soul passions. Todd had done this for me. I wanted to do it for others.

A chill rushed through me with a clear knowing: *This is why I am here.*